Path Finder

A Guide for the Newly Awakened

COVID-19 Edition

For you, your family and community, and for the Earth

Johnny Peaceseed

Edited by John Elmer Lee

ESSENTIAL PRESS

info@johnnypeaceseed.org
johnnypeaceseed.org
Copyright © 2020 John Elmer Lee
All Rights Reserved

ISBN Number 978-1-887555-06-7

Dedication

Path Finder: COVID-19 Edition is dedicated to all those awakening to the current and imminent crises before us and for those ready to help turn the course of humanity from blind belief and self-aggrandizement to the recognition that all of the species on this earth are necessary to our survival, and we for theirs, *even SARS-CoV-2* .

Without the COVID-19 wake-up call we may have continued down the road to ineffectively dealing with the multiple crises and disasters that are all coming due now. We may have continued following many utterly incompetent "leaders" to our possible extinction. If we set a new course, we have a chance. For us to succeed, we can no longer use the tools that got us here. We must now create new ways to organize ourselves, new leaders to guide us who don't rely on unfounded belief and self-aggrandizement. As we no longer use stone axes to cut down trees, we must stop following stone age leaders, who only know bullying, who lead through emotional and physical intimidation, and who live dreams of domination.

To start our journey, we must go back in time and look at how we got to this state of affairs. Then, we can let go the beliefs and behaviours that have kept us repeating history for over fifty thousand years.

This book was written because my wife Constance told me I must. So Constance, I have tried to honor your wishes by writing with more love than upset, more kindness than judgment, and with more certainty that we humans will finally let go the mistakes of our species' youth, and find our way to balance.

Path Finder is also dedicated to my sons Jason and Matthew who taught me that opening your heart is far better than any lessons taught or learned. And to my grandsons Simon and Rubus, yet to find their paths in life, it is my fervent hope that this book, in some small way, will lead to a better world for you, and all those searching for purpose and meaning in their lives.

Finally, this book is dedicated to Greta Thunberg and all those now leading the way.

Table of Contents

Dedication	iii
About Path Finder	7
Disclaimers	11
Prologue	13

CHAPTER ONE
The Spoken World — 17

Language	18
The Spoken and Written World	23
The Linear Mind	25
Lies	28
Leaders	31
Leaders and Elites	33
Homo Sapiens?	36
Two Analogies	41

CHAPTER TWO
To Be Awakened — 43

Triggers	51

CHAPTER THREE
Principles — 61

Your Principles	70
First Principles	72

CHAPTER FOUR
Practices — 77
Taking Control — 78
Acting on Your Practices — 80
Every Moment is a Meditation — 82

CHAPTER FIVE
Path Finder — 83
Flying Solo — 84
Finding Your Path — 93
Path Finder — 97
Steps to Change the World — 102

Epilogue — 107
The Awakened World — 108

ACKNOWLEDGEMENTS
My Three Muses — 113

ABOUT
John Elmer Lee — 115
A Brief History — 115

ABOUT
Johnny Peaceseed — 117
Johnny's Awakening — 118
Johnny's Perfect World — 120

About Path Finder
COVID-19 Edition

Well, another fine mess we have gotten into. We are now teetering on the edge of another abyss, with more existential threats rapidly approaching. We have been moving toward these threats for over fifty thousand years, and now all of our species past missteps have converged. This is how we got here:

Meta-History

Lexico.com definition of Meta-History:
Inquiry into the principles governing historical events; the study of the philosophy of history, or of historiography; specifically the study of the structure of historical narrative.

Path Finder definition of Meta-History:
The underlying causes and actions that govern human behavior. When we say, "history repeats itself," we are saying that the behaviors and beliefs we have developed, both as individuals, and as communities, will ensure similar outcomes in similar situations. To those asleep in the behaviors and beliefs systems anything beyond this is invisible. Those behaviors and beliefs are all they see. It is their universe.

It is only by examining the *meta-history* of the world that we can find answers to address the coming deluge, so that we don't ever "repeat history" again. This cycle can only be broken by breaking free of those past behaviours and beliefs. That can only happen if we "wake up," and step outside the constraints of the behaviours and beliefs that have limited our connection to being present and in the moment. It is then we can choose awakened leaders, become awakened followers, or become awakened leaders ourselves. We have over fifty thousands years of history to overcome, but we will succeed. To fail is the end of humankind.

This is a time-line of our species' history and how we got to this point:
1. We started with unfounded belief created through the invention of language between fifty and one hundred thousand years ago.
2. Second was the beginning of species extinctions tens of millennia ago as humanity left the plains of Africa and spread across the Earth.
3. Third was the cultural shift from nomadic tribes to settled agricultural communities around ten millennia ago.
4. Fourth was the invention of "civilization," the mass control of communities for the benefit of elites, around five millennia ago.
5. Fifth was the human caused weather interventions, including the little ice age, starting in sixteenth century.
6. Sixth was rapid expansion of human populations and the rapid conversion of natural habitats to farming and human population centers of the last five-hundred years.
7. Seventh was the rapid industrialization and expanded international trade, especially in the last two hundred years, and the beginnings of global warming.

8. Eighth was the planetary pollution and the poisoning of the biosphere of the last one hundred years.
9. Ninth with the invention and use of nuclear weapons seventy-five years ago.
10. Tenth was the intermingling of global human communities and the rise of new disease vectors as the human race put its footprint on the last bits of virgin forest, jungles, wetland and in the deep oceans in the last seventy years.
11. Eleventh was the rise of human caused epidemics, from HIV to Ebola to SARS to MERS to COVID-19 in the last fifty years.
12. Twelfth is human caused Global Warming and the existential devastation now before us.

Today, we must the start the long recovery process and reverse the voracious destruction of our home, or we will continue headlong over the cliff of unenlightened self-interest, blind greed, willful ignorance, and subservience to narcissistic sociopaths that we, willingly or unwillingly, chose to follow for tens of thousands of years.

To all the awakened seekers in the world, now is the time for action. Understanding the history of the human race, and developing powerful principles and practices will allow you to take meaningful action and to join with others on the path of restoration of the Earth. You know what is needed. Now is the time to put your dreams into action.

Johnny Peaceseed, April 4, 2020

Disclaimers

Disclaimer One

Listen to your awakened mind and follow the advice it gives you. Your awakened mind knows more about your needs than any book could, but if Path Finder offers a glimmer of recognition, or if it serves you to build upon your awakening, that is all that matters. Also, please ignore all mentions of Johnny Peaceseed if it obscures your the understanding of the information found in this book. Johnny is merely a literary device to describe the intuitive part of my brain that, while critical to my awakening, is not easily described. If you are still interested in knowing more about Johnny Peaceseed, please read the last section of this book about his life and times.

Disclaimer Two

I am not a guru. I am not a spiritual leader, and I have absolutely no interest in creating a cult. I am just someone who found purpose in my life and have chosen to share what I learned. You will have to find your guru elsewhere. You might even find, that upon awakening, your guru was with you all along, awaiting you. If that is the case, say hello to your heart and intuitive mind.

Disclaimer Three

This book is *not* James Fenimore Cooper's *"The Pathfinder."* Please go back to the bookstore, or library, and exchange this book for Cooper's book, if that is what you seek. This book, *"Path Finder: COVID-19 Edition,"* is not a novel. It was written in 2020, not 1840. This book could be categorized as a self-help book, or a guide book, or maybe a call to personal action. It may be, like Cooper's book, a tale for the adventurous.

Prologue

"Believe those who are seeking the truth; doubt those who find it."
— André Gide

Awakening

Path Finder is meant for those who are awakened, or nearly awakened, from the slumber of belief and dogma, and for those who seek their full potential. The title of this book refers to your journey to find meaning and purpose in your life, and is meant to help you gain clarity when undertaking your journey of self-discovery. It is not meant to tell you what to think, or not to think, but it may touch on how to think. What comes after that is up to you. Path Finder will also help you to enlarge upon your awakening, and will assist you to develop principles and practices to guide your journey.

In this book there are teachings found in Christianity, Buddhism, and Sufism, as well as secular books of wisdom. I have taken freely from the words of saints, while avoiding dogma not related to those words. The filter was a life of learning, my heart and my intuition.

"At times you have to leave the city of your comfort and go into the wilderness of your intuition. What you'll discover will be wonderful. What you'll discover is yourself."

~ Alan Alda

In order to take advantage of your awakening, it will be necessary that you honor *all* of your intentions and your commitments, no matter where that may lead you. To be powerful, the awakened also must also act with integrity in all that they do. Honor is not an abstract concept, that you can be honorable only when it is convenient or comfortable. If you are not willing to fully honor your intentions and commitments, you have not truly awakened, and you will surely fail at whatever path you have chosen.

> "The spiritual journey is individual, highly personal. It can't be organized or regulated. It isn't true that everyone should follow one path. Listen to your own truth."
>
> ~ Ram Das

When awakened, you are capable of leading an intentional, committed and loving life. When awakened, you are able to accomplish great good. When awakened, you are able to make a real difference in other people's lives. The reward will not be the keys to heaven, or even the admiration of others. The reward is power. Power over yourself. Power to choose. Power to serve. Power to join others who also serve. When awakened, you have access to the deepest joy. You also have access the deepest emotional pain, and the full expression of it. Pain, fully felt and expressed, is your ally though, because expressing and releasing emotional pain opens you to unconditional love. Those already awakened are now your closest family. Serving the awakenings of others is now your calling. Hearts healing hearts, and perhaps more.

> "To serve is beautiful, but only if it is done with joy and a whole heart and a free mind."
>
> ~ Pearl S. Buck

CHAPTER ONE
The Spoken World

"There are ten parts of speech and they are all troublesome."
∼ Mark Twain

Language

Early humans were able to communicate before the invention of written and spoken language using facial expressions, gestures, body languages, touch, vocalizations and chemical signaling, *e.g. I'm ovulating.* Using these communications they could express joy, happiness, sadness, anger, fear, danger, attraction, tenderness, concern, food or predator location and more. Without spoken or written language though, our ancestors were limited in their ability to transfer more·complex information using these limited method of communications to others in their tribe.

For instance, it would be difficult to tell your tribe the exact location of a food source, or where a predator lay hidden. Only if the food or predator was in close proximity could you share that information. It would be much more difficult if the food or predator was ten kilometers away. With the invention of language, early humans were able to communicate much more effectively, and in much greater detail, than was previously possible. Language allowed our ancestors to share descriptions of the world, and to share information about the needs of daily life: food preparation, tool making, hunting, foraging, shelter building, etc.

Some of the information that was transmitted was the retelling of events that members of the tribe had witnessed. Stories about hunts, battles with nature, mighty leaders, births and deaths and inexplicable happenings. These stories were repeated many times, and also passed down to each new generation. At some point the stories transmuted beyond the simple re-tellings of events. Through countless repetitions, the information was embellished, and through the embellishments, the stories gained greater significance.

Over time, the stories became myths, and came to be believed as true reckonings of the tribe's history, and to define the tribe. These myths were cohesive and deepened the tribe's bonds.

Myth
Dictionary Definition:
A usually traditional story of ostensibly historical events that serves to unfold part of the world view of a people or explain a practice, belief, or natural phenomenon.

"Belief, myth and dogma are the spoken world's controllers and limiters of human behavior. They regulate communities and the people within them, stifle creativity, suppress imagination, and narrow discourse."
~ *Johnny Peaceseed, Momentary Memoirs*

The Inexplicable
Seeking answers to mysteries and the inexplicable, humans used language to create new myths; myths that invented gods and spirits, magic and sorcery, rituals and incantations, and the reading of tea leaves and stars. For the tribe's members the myths of magic and sorcery became another lens through which the tribe viewed much of their world. Along with the myths of the tribe's history, the myths of gods and devils came to hold sway, and to become the dogma that further united the tribe. As a result, over tens of thousands of years, language strengthened the bonds of human communities, and allowed the people within them to work together in greater and greater numbers, and to build larger and larger communities.

Dogma
Dictionary Definition:
A point of view or tenet put forth as authoritative without adequate grounds.

The underpinnings of the lives of early humans slowly shifted from directly experiencing the world, to experiencing the world through beliefs and the constructs of belief where the description of reality is turned into an imperfect clone of reality. The beliefs solidified into myths, and finally into dogma over time, and become the cultural glue that defined the tribe's world, just as our myths, and our dogma, define our world today. In this world, they began to build new myths and dogma, new allegiances, larger groups, then towns, cities and nations.

A Search for Understanding
In trying to understand the nature of the world, early humans had begun the long search for knowledge that eventually, millennia later, led to the invention of the scientific method. For most of human history since the invention of language, and long before the scientific revolution, myths, and the joining and conjoining of myths played a greater and greater role in how humans interacted with the world. After tens of thousands of years the myths, dogma, and other inventions of language gave humans an advantage over other predators. They could work together in greater numbers, share knowledge more readily and develop new technologies, such as the transitions from stone, to copper, to bronze and to iron tools.

Their new power came with a high price, though. Living their lives in the world of language, myths and dogma, they would have found difficulty directly experiencing the natural world due to the inherent nature of language's linear underpinnings. As humans became less reliant on their personal connection to what their senses actually experienced, they came to rely more on language and the dictates of belief to give them direction. Their beliefs, founded and unfounded, came to dominate their world. The underpinnings of the lives of early humans slowly shifted from directly experiencing the world, to experiencing the world through belief and the constructs of belief, where the description of reality is turned into an imperfect clone of reality, and where today, most of us now live out our lives. The pseudo-reality we live in now includes empires, both corporate and political, rules of law, doctrines of good and evil, the dictates of theology and society, who we are allowed to love and who we must hate. Buddhists call this state Maya, a world lived in illusion.

Everyday Stories

Beyond the myths and dogma inherent in all societies, there are the everyday stories that we are told and that we tell ourselves. These stories give meaning to our lives, as well as becoming templates of what we should expect out of life. We have all grown up with these stories inculcated by parents, teachers, friends, other members of our community, and through written materials, movies, television, songs and now the internet. Odes to great adventures or great endurance. Songs of exceptional loves and of love's demise. Stories that define for us beauty and ugliness, whether *we* are beautiful or *we* are ugly, and to what degree. Fairy tales and allegories. Stories of whom we should love and whom we should hate. Stories of enmities that lead us to war, and sometimes to peace. Tales that define us, and let us, through words and images, and our imaginations, to indirectly experience life.

These everyday stories have been our contact highs, where we are allowed to have a pseudo-experience of what real life feels like. Stories our asleep hearts yearn to hear. Yet these stories help to keep us as asleep as any dogma. They keep us asleep because they are not our experiences, nor our truths. They speak not from our hearts, but from another's.

The Spoken and Written World

The World of Belief

"Belief only allows you to travel in a straight line. You may know all that is exactly in front of you, or exactly behind you. Do not look to the side; you will be lost. If you travel at the direction of your heart, all that is straight ahead, and all that is not, becomes your universe."

~ *Johnny Peaceseed*

We have been deeply enmeshed in the spoken and written world for almost all of our lives, and unless awakened, until the day we die. A world of words and belief. The spoken world, can describe existence in great detail, but it is not the experience of existence. Language can describe a belief, but the belief is not truth, only a description of something that might, or might not be true. Saying the word love, is not the same as feeling love. Language can describe emotions, but the language used is not the emotion it describes. We forget that love is not found in the language of love, it is found in our hearts and minds. Love and good exist without the need for language, without the intervention of any fantasy stories, and are not derived from some emperor's musings deep within the spoken world. At its best, language permits highly detailed transmissions of information between members of our species, and, to a lesser degree, with other species. At its worst, language, and unfounded belief, enslave us.

The world of belief, myth and dogma was created so long ago that most of us have forgotten that it is just made up from inventions of language. Humanity came to rely on these inventions to such a degree, that people started to live their lives inside these fabricated worlds, and as they did, they started to lose connection with their direct experience of each moment. The creation of unfounded belief, myth and dogma became the first great failure of humanity. Today, the inventions of the spoken world are, for most of us, almost all that exists.

I wonder if the whales have a similar world of song, or if they have managed, in creating their songs, to avoid myth and belief. Or are they as disconnected as we? From each other, from their hearts, from their awareness of the moment. If so, that would make a whale of a sad tale.

The Linear Mind

"The linear mind is like a monkey riding a dog, and you're the dog."

~ Johnny Peaceseed

Your linear language mind loves to pretend it knows it all. This is a fundamental attribute of belief. *"Living the dream,"* and willing to ignore any evidence contrary to the stories it thrives upon, especially if the evidence is contrary to our selfish impulses. So, for the believer, and especially for the true believer, the intuitive mind slowly moves into the background, only to become a suppressed reminder of the inadequacy of the limited world a belief allows.

Linearity

Linearity of thought, as is required by the constructs of language, makes it very nearly impossible to make well thought out decisions. If one does not fully understand all the ramifications of a problem, and all its complexity, any attempt to find a solution will almost certainly lead to less than ideal results, and may actually make the problem worse. Linear thinking, along with unexamined belief, has played a huge role in almost all of the follies humans have undertaken throughout history. Multiple or conjoined beliefs have the potential to create havoc far greater than any single belief could. The reliance on linear thinking, and the suppression of the global thinking intuitive mind was the second great failure of humanity. See the Fenn diagram below for an example of conjoined beliefs, *and please pardon my bias:*

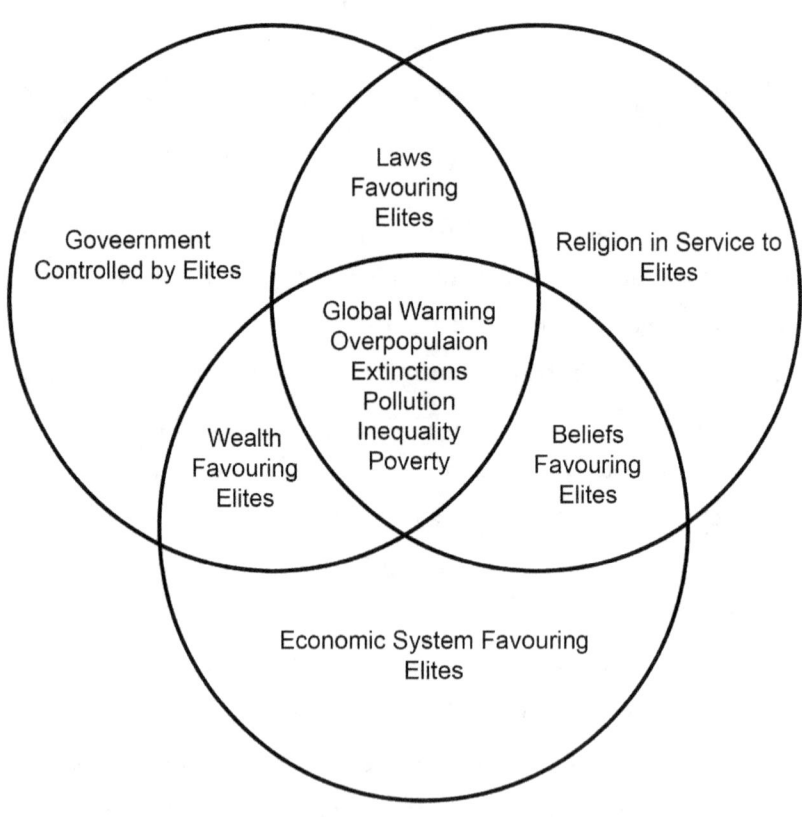

In the linear mind of belief there are two uniting principles that hold societies and groups of people together. The first is the development of community, the bonding together of groups by means of common agreements, beliefs, hopes, values and shared experience. The second is the sharing of common enemies and common fears.

One or both of these may lead to more cohesive societies. One brings internal agreement about what is, and is not to be believed by the community, dependent upon their myths and dogma. The other teaches whom to fear or hate. Neither gives a true picture of the worth of that which they approve or that which they disapprove. They become closed systems, both for those within, and to those without. The largest vulnerabilities they face are the dangers that lurk outside their belief systems. The things they do not know they do not know. Over that, they have no awareness and no control.

Lies

"Who are you going to believe, me, or your lying eyes."
   ~ *Chico Marx, Dorothy Dix, et al*

Deception and Self Deception

After the great failures of unfounded belief and linear thinking, comes the third great failure of lies, the lies of individuals, the lies of the community's elites, the lies about the community's posed enemies, and the lies we tell ourselves.

Children

Lying starts soon after speech develops in the very young. Lies, at that early age, are seen as protectants by the young child when suspected of disobeying rules, such as eating something that has been forbidden. Fear of punishment, or parental disappointment, heightens the likelihood of a dishonest response.

As the child gets older, the habituation to lying is passed, back and forth, between younger siblings, relatives and friends. Sometimes the lies are shared, when more that one child feels the need for protection. This can lead to escalating battles and recriminations between parent and child, that may last well past childhood. In schools, the same pattern is repeated. The child learns that, to get along, they must conform with their group's likes and prejudices, as well as the challenges of rote learning and subservience. They may subsume their personal values, and yield to the group thinking of their peers and their teachers. The lie here, is to themselves.

In young adulthood, the lying continues, but with even more import. What is at stake now are romantic relationships, scholastic and athletic achievements, the child's fit in the social life of their school and their parent's expectations. Getting caught cheating, going against their parents wishes, or exhibiting antisocial behavior, either at school or within their peer relationships, can have dire consequences. As when they were younger, lying continues to be the prime avenue to escape responsibility for their actions.

By the time they are ready to go to college or enter the work world most young adults are polished prevaricators. They can lie without showing outward emotion to family, friends, and partners. Before I go any further, I must point out that not all children, or young adults follow this path. Religious training, and strict parenting may make some too fearful to lie. Permissive parents, willing to give in to the their child's impulses may also avoid having to deal with a prevaricating child. Neither of these choices serves the child all that well. Only if the parents have the time and inclination to give the child adequate love and attention, can there be any hope of avoiding punishments and other means of coercion. In a sane society, with time for proper parenting and ongoing bonding, that becomes much more likely.

Criminals

Elites are seldom punished for their crimes, and only then if they become an embarrassment to their peers. The elites are protected by laws and militias, the lack of enforcement by police and by buying their way out of trouble. The community members, without the protections that wealth and power make available to the elites, have the choice to either accept the constraints placed upon them by the community, or to willfully act out their selfish impulses, and either face the consequences of their choices, or out of the fear of getting caught, lie to protect themselves. If they are successful in avoiding punishment, they are vindicated, and may again push the limits of the community. They may become habitual liars. They may not feel remorseful because they are just doing what their peers do. If they do feel guilt, it likely leads to more resentment of the cultural norms. Thus, the criminal mind is born.

Elites

The elites, in almost all communities, develop systems where the elites gain most of the benefits of the community, but this is hidden from the society though lies, half truths, and misrepresentation of facts. The elites produce propaganda touting their concern for all community members, but to the most selfish of the elites, the non-elites are little more than cheap labor, or lives to be manipulated.

Posing Enemies

In countries as diverse as India and the United States, citizens are frequently propagandized and taught to disrespect the lower classes, people of color, different religions, sexual identifications, immigrants, and citizens of other countries. People living in, or from other countries may even be posed as enemies of the state. Internal outbreaks of abuse and hate crimes are the result. Internationally, wars may be fought over territory, trade routes, or for resources, but they are not fought over ideals, and ways of life. Yet that is the reason given for almost all the wars in the last one hundred years. If the elites said, they are declaring war because they would love dominate a new batch of people, and steal the resources of those people to enrich themselves, there would be fewer recruits. But if the elites say a war is fought because they are, for example, bringing democracy or religion to a land of heathens, the citizens will clamour to wrap themselves with flags and sign-up. The elite's dreams of domination come to pass and the nightmares of those being led to war come to pass as well.

"If you tell the truth, you don't have to remember anything."
~ Mark Twain

Leaders

Early Leaders

"Be careful of living your life based only on faith and signs, or you might find yourself standing in a South American jungle holding a glass of Kool-Aid."

~ Shannon L. Alder

Before language, our early ancestors chose the same type of leaders that we choose today. In the near and distant past, and today, the most aggressive humans most often rose to the top. The difference between then and now is that the bullying that leaders used in ancient times was mostly physical. Now, the bullying is mostly verbal and psychological, but the threat of physical aggression is always present. From bullying parents to bullying media to bullying presidents.

With the invention of language, occasionally a member of the tribe rose to leadership who best told stories that conformed to the dogma of their community, or one who could convince the most aggressive to follow them.

Occasionally, modern humans choose leaders based on their intellect, wisdom, and compassion; ones who broke through the then current paradigm. Since the advent of language, these leaders have been rare exceptions.

And this is the fourth great failure of humanity. Prior to spoken language, this was not an issue because the tribes were too small to do irreparable damage. For the last several millennia though, using the power of language and belief, self-aggrandizing leaders have come to control the behavior of, first hundreds then thousands, then millions, and today billions of humans.

Gods and Dominion

As we look at the rapid expansion of humanity across the world one could argue that it is our genes that are the cause, that we are programmed to bow to authoritarian leaders, just as we are driven to procreate and follow a biological imperative to multiply. The dogmas preached in the past said the gods, and goddesses gave the leaders the divine right to rule, just as they gave them the right to dominion over their subjects, and over the birds and the beasts. Today, there are no divine rights giving leaders the right to lead.

Embedding Belief

What has changed over the last few thousand years is the addition of more deeply embedded beliefs in larger portions of humanity, whether administered by warlords, kings, dictators, or by *"democracies"* controlled by elites. In the past the leaders *were* the elites. Today, it is not as clearly defined. There may still be powerful kings, or sultans in a few places, and there are still dictators leading authoritarian governments, although many of these are merely puppets of the more powerful countries that keep them in power. The last great invention in crowd control, democracy, was meant to persuade people to think their vote counts. And of course their vote does count, but almost always to decide which of the bickering elites will be in control, from local governments to the capitals of the world. As with earlier systems of subjection, people in democracies are controlled by belief, dogma and the constructs of language. Different system than before, but the same result.

Leaders and Elites

"The liberty of a democracy is not safe if the people tolerate the growth of private power to a point where it becomes stronger than their democratic state itself. That, in its essence, is fascism - ownership of government by an individual, by a group or by any controlling private power."

~ Franklin Delano Roosevelt

In *democratic* societies, the elites almost always put up *"leaders"* for us to choose, leaders that will do the bidding of the elites. Not really leaders, rather uber-followers serving the elite's bidding. Occasionally someone will rise who is not beholden to the elites, but they are a minority.

Few of the elites today are prime ministers, or presidents, or politicians. The elites in modern democracies are usually the most privileged and wealthiest, the billionaires, the corporate owners, the military heads, the criminal syndicate heads, the financiers, and those who control voting blocks. The elites rule through *"owning"* politicians, subterfuge and propaganda. They are the ones who write the laws concerning taxation, corporate rules, limits on environmental protections, political expenditures, and the movement of money. They are the ones who choose whom we are to hate and fear. They are puppeteers in the sleeping world, and we sleeping billions have been trapped within their cruel dreams. All of us sharing the elite's dreams, every man, woman, and child, only from vastly differing perspectives.

We can no longer participate in the dreams of oil barons, bankers, corporate raiders, self-serving preachers, and all those in service to the elite's whims. Our belief that narcissists and sociopaths could lead the way is at an end. If we left the choice of who will next lead us to the elites, it would likely mean the end of human civilization, and the acceleration of the sixth great extinction. It is unlikely, nay nearly impossible, that keeping the same autocratic leaders in power would lead to humanities' golden age. Rather, the opposite. There is no evidence that the elites currently in power will be able turn the tide, nor those they choose next for us. Their myths and dogma are too firmly lodged inside their closed minds, while we are finally letting go the myths of subservience altogether. The days of dominion, of privilege, of autocratic rule have finally come to an end

The Fifth and Final Great Failure

The fifth great failure of humanity is the destruction and dismantling of the natural world over the last ten thousand years, all in the name of *"progress."* The poisoning of the environment, species extinctions, global warming and runaway overpopulation must be addressed. The elites whose names, and whose dreams, are written of in the histories of nations, and those who are glorified on the statuary and the edifices in the capitals of the world are the cause. They are the engines for the fifth great failure. It is they, and their asleep dreams and nightmares that have failed. It has been we and the Earth that has suffered.

Incompetence, Malfeasance and Dishonesty

We can start to extricate ourselves from the elite's dreams by reconnecting to our environment, our communities and our families. In the elite's dream we have become so inured to incompetence, malfeasance and dishonesty. When we don't experience them we are shocked and surprised. Competence and honesty seem too good to be true. It is more important to the elites that we be good consumers and servants than it is to notice the poverty, and suffering all around us. In the elite's dream charisma and looking good are more important then substance and quality of character. We learned to expect little of those around us and less of ourselves.

So, as we awaken, we change our daily routines to bring back joy to our lives. Maybe we could start our day by reading poetry until we learn how to cry again. Or start helping those around us until the ability to fully feel compassion is restored. Perhaps we can start reading internet news sources from around the world until we can see shades of grey, instead of just black and white. We can start connecting with our families and friends until we have the ability to fully love once more. We can teach others the simple lessons we learned. And finally, we can join with others to end poverty, to end war, to stop pandemics before they savage our lives, to reverse global warming, to end all the scourges the elites have brought upon us. Then, we can begin to turn the tide.

"In a room where people unanimously maintain a conspiracy of silence, one word of truth sounds like a pistol shot."
~ Czesław Miłosz

Homo Sapiens?

"We must perform cleansing rites. Make the necessary sacrifices. We must replant our huge trees that have been uprooted, replenish our sacred forests that have been decimated."
— Véronique Tadjo, As the Crow Flies

Homo Credula

While stories myths and dogma allowed humans to build larger communities, it came at a heavy price, and it is a price we pay today. Our ancestors accepted unfounded belief and dogma as truth. This meant more people working together, although with many, against their will. What our ancestors gave up was living in the present. In doing so, they became what I shall call, *Homo Credula,* the gullible species. By developing language humans learned how to describe their world, to tell stories about their world, to believe those stories, and finally to use those stories to mostly replace their direct connection with the natural world.

Despite their limitations, belief, myth and dogma took hold because of their ability to control human behavior. They were ideally suited to ambitious leaders seeking domination of those beneath them. The dogmas developed through language, made entirely from a community's shared beliefs, allowed early humans to spread across the globe, to *"conquer"* the natural world, and to supplant any species that got in the way.

Unfounded belief, dogma, and other trickeries of language made possible the building of larger and larger communities of shared belief, allowed great cities to be built, allowed wars to be fought, allowed emperors and kings to dominate greater and greater numbers of humans. All through the hypnotic power of shared beliefs and dogma.

Homo Exstinctor

When belief became dogma it solidified into rigid societal constraints. As humans expanded out of Africa into new territories, they proceeded to kill most of the large herbivores and carnivores they found, while they proceeded to drive their near relatives to extinction, until humans became the lone apex predator of the Earth.

As our species spread, they destroyed the habitability of huge swathes of the earth, built and destroyed civilizations and damaged the natural world wherever they wandered. The great population explosion of humanity spread to every continent, and with the spread, the extermination of millions of species, the pollution of the natural world, and the beginnings of human-driven global warming. Today, humans could be better named *Homo Exstinctor*, the exterminating species.

All of this from our shared languages, beliefs and dogma. We, each of us, along with all of our human brothers and sisters, created, or went along with, the narratives that defined our species. The invention of language is not at fault for the current state of affairs. Instead, it is our abuse of language's promise to help in the communication of knowledge. Instead of using language to provide us with better understanding of the world, we created fantasy worlds of dominion, subjugation and separation to divide us from each other, and from the natural world. For that, belief is squarely at fault. And that means that it is we who are responsible. And it is we who must provide restitution.

A Partial List of Human Caused Crises

Worldwide Crises:

One million species at risk
- Reduced habitat
- Pollution
- Predation
- Invasive species

The Earth in crisis
- Temperatures rising
- Glaciers melting
- Rising seas
- Desertification
- Poison on the land and in the seas

Humanity in crisis
- COVID-19
  Starvation
- Poverty
- Inequality
- Arable land failing
- Living conditions degrading
- Wars for resources
- Wars for control
- Overpopulation

For those awakening it has become impossible to believe the stories and myths and propaganda in our lives, when we can so clearly see that they are not true. It is harder to buy into pyramid schemes of riches, harder to find meaning through buying the latest fashions, or the newest cars. We can no longer feel validated by joining the right clique, group, fraternity, gang or religion. We are not satisfied with all our likes on social media. We are no longer willing to be just another product of a corporation selling our identity to the highest bidder. We are no longer able to accept that myths define us as Joseph Campbell suggested.

We weep at the legacy of humanity's blind ambition, and blind belief, as corrupt politicians, oligarchs, generals and talking heads generate more dream enemies for humanity to hate, but we can no longer find respite behind the walls of gated communities, and gated minds. We can no longer find respite in *la vida loca*, the adrenalized life. We can no longer numb ourselves with alcohol, drugs and electronic distractions. We can no longer listen to the cacophony of lies reverberating in our heads. Enough is enough.

Homo Restorus

The dream state that ninety-nine percent of the human race has been in for tens of thousands of years has left our world in tatters, but the ramparts of unfounded belief and dogma are beginning to crumble. The dogmas that try to deny our presence in each moment are cracking wide open, and are unable to stop or filter the leakages of reality. The Earth is in crisis. Welcome *Homo Restorus*.

Beginning Days

Given past experience, one might think these could be the end of days, but they definitely are not. These are the beginning days. Due to humanity's past failures, the Earth is in flux, but humanity is finally, finally awakening. Humanity is starting to see without the blinders that belief has placed over our hearts and minds. The young, and those most affected, are starting the call to action. Their wisest elders are eagerly joining them. Humanity is undergoing a transformation as great as the end of the dinosaurs.

All that is left to be done is to wake the rest of our brothers and sisters. Some of what lies ahead will be easy, and some will be very difficult. No matter how great the effort that is required of us, we will not be deterred from bringing forth the next stage in human evolution, to welcome *Homo Restorus*, the restorer, as our successor, or to at least be worthy of the name *Homo Sapiens*.

Awakening to Leadership

At no time in human history has the need for awakened selfless, wise leadership been greater. The threats before us are too great to leave to the current elites. The leadership of the entitled, privileged elites is completely inadequate to address all that their choices have wrought. It is time for humanity to face the reality of those choices, and fearlessly challenge them.

Listening to the elite's tired exculpations of denial about the decline of species, about the pollution of the Earth and the threats of global warming has finally worn thin. It is awakened humanity who shall now choose those who will lead. A great change is underway. People are awakening, and willing to take action. For them, sleep is no longer an option, nor is hand wringing or inaction.

Two Analogies
A Computer Analogy

"Unfounded belief is, without doubt, the greatest coding error humans ever devised. It has led to more suffering by more people, and more species, in more places, and in more times, that all other human failings combined."

~ Johnny Peaceseed, Momentary Memoirs

The human mind's functioning could be seen as analogous to how a computer solves equations. In this analogy, the programmer is your linear language mind and the central processing unit (cpu) is the global thinking intuitive mind. The programmer (the linear mind) sends code (words) to the cpu (intuitive mind), where it then processes the data and returns a result (the conclusion).

If the data that is sent is unreliable (unfounded belief) or incorrect (lies), it is treated exactly the same as reliable data, unless there is a filtering mechanism to ignore or bypass the unreliable or incorrect code. The filtering is analogous to the intuitive mind's deception detecting abilities.

If the intuitive mind is not fully available, due to the linear mind filtering access through rigid assumptions e.g. dogma, or other means, the intuitive mind can only process what remains. The computer term for this is *garbage in, garbage out.*

If the brain circuitry is damaged or faulty, either physically or through embedded faulty assumptions, and cannot process the data correctly it will return poor or incorrect conclusions. This is analogous to some forms of mental illness.

Note: Without the intervention of the linear mind, the intuitive mind receives data directly from our senses as well, and can act on it. This data comes directly via all the sensory inputs, and can bypass the data sent through the language circuitry. Thus, it can bypass most programming errors.

A problem occurs when the reliance on the linear mind causes a strengthening of the circuitry from the senses to the linear mind, and a diminishment of the circuitry for the senses direct connection to the intuitive mind. This started to happen when humans first began using language. The linear mind, as it built the world of dogma and unfounded belief, also slowly began to suppress the filters, the error correction mechanisms of the intuitive mind, until they no longer played a major part in much of the thought processes. The computer term for this is *buggy*.

A Firearms Analogy

"Using unfounded belief in your decision making is like playing Russian Roulette. Sooner or later, the weapon will fire."
~ Johnny Peaceseed, *Momentary Memoirs*

CHAPTER TWO
To Be Awakened

"Awakening is to be reborn with your memories intact, but with a new heart."

~ *Johnny Peaceseed*

"Awakening is about liberating yourself from the prison that is the world of the mind and daring to be here as all that you are."

~ Leonard Jacobson

To Be Awakened

May I be open to learning,
may my heart be found true,
may I let go unfounded belief,
and erroneous view.

May I let go selfish impulse,
and let go personal gain,
when afraid, may I find solace,
when suffering, may I accept pain.
May I love without limits,
and in my actions be kind,
heart without fear,
seeking hearts to join mine,
finding my peace,
in troublesome times.

May we all be awakened.
may we be alive and set free,
to humbly seek knowledge,
and embrace harmony.

May we all be as one,
may we all be renewed,
hearts in the moment,
to seek only good.

Goodbye to brooding and moods,
and shoulds, woulds, and coulds.
Welcome peace and forgiveness,
and hearts understood.

Some Definitions

"I wish to weep but sorrow is stupid. I wish to believe but belief is a graveyard."

~ *Charles Bukowski*

Belief
Dictionary Definition:
A state or habit of mind in which trust or confidence is placed in some person or thing.

Path Finder definition:
Belief in the attributes of a gods, myths or dogma.

Becoming Your Heart
Path Finder definition:
You will find the term becoming your heart scattered around this book. I tried finding a definition for "becoming your heart," but I could not find anything in Merriam Webster or other dictionaries. Nothing in WebMD either, so all I have to offer is my own personal definition. Becoming your heart is where your life and all your actions are under the control of your heart, your heart chakra, your compassionate center, whatever part of you that is mediated by love. In practice, this means everything in your life becomes an act of compassion; your work, your play, your relationships, everything.

Linear Thinking
Path Finder definition:
Linear Thinking, sometimes called analytical thinking, refers to thought originating through spoken or written language alone, and is found in the left side of the brain where belief also resides. Linear

thinking follows a series of steps, each one leading to the next. Glimpses of global thinking may be had by interjections of information, outside the linear thinking process as in a movie that bounces back and forth between past and present. For one seeing life as a series of linear processes, this may lead to confusion, and may make the understanding of complex ideas a fruitless endeavor. A person, reliant on linear thinking alone, may be unable to process complex thoughts, and are more likely to founder inside the world of stories, belief, myth and dogma. Lineal thinking is limited by the constraints of language, and must rely on the linear process alone, where the intuitive part of the mind is seen only as a dimly lit conscience, or may be as a momentary glimpse of something hidden behind an opaque curtain.

Global Thinking
Path Finder definition:
Global Thinking resides in the right side of the brain, the side where emotion also lives. For the purposes of this book the terms Intuition and Global Thinking are mostly synonymous, although intuition is perhaps just a large subset of the global thinking mind. The person who thinks globally sees the world in a much richer fashion, where more of the mind is used in the processing of information. Relying less on language and more on the brain's ability to process many threads of information at once, much more complex ideation is possible.

Global thinking gives greater access to creative thinking, and is not deeply attached to belief, myth and dogma, and in fact, is much better able to discern fallacies in such thoughts. In past times, global thinkers such as Jesus Christ were killed, because they pointed out the fallacy of the beliefs of the day, or were made to recant their knowledge, as was Galileo.

To simplify these definitions, one could say that the linear thinker's world is the world seen as a description, whereas the global thinker's world is the world being witnessed. The linear thinking mind is where impulsive decisions, poor judgment, not looking before you leap, gullibility, narrow views, and belief live. The global thinking mind is where greater comprehension, love, compassion, and self awareness make their home.

When the linear thinking mind is running the show, love is not the experience of an emotion. The linear mind can only provide a description of the emotion, and it is clouded by likes and dislikes, fears and misunderstanding, self-involvement and self-interest. When the global thinking intuitive mind is in charge, love is a direct expression of the heart, a gift given without expectation or restraint.

Advice and Caveats

Communication

If you are fluent at thinking globally, take care with your communication, if you do not wish to have Jesus Christ's or Galileo's fate befall you. If you are going to transmit information meant for both linear and global thinkers first break it down to a level that a linear thinking person might be able to comprehend. Either that, or divide your message and audiences, so that both may understand at the level they are capable. Many of us have felt the sting of not abiding by either of these choices. This is the reason that, in the good old days, speaking of transmuting lead into gold was code for becoming enlightened.

Forgiveness

Linear thinkers are not to blame for the calamities of the world. Language and unfounded belief are the culprits. Forgive those asleep when they go astray or become confused in this complex world we all created. Remember, at some point you too, relied mostly on linear thinking. You have found, or are in the process of finding, a way to free yourself from this imagined world. If you are awakened, and have left unfounded belief behind, please offer compassion and kindness to those still asleep. Please forgive them their sins. They know not what they do. Recognizing this, you may now follow your path to undo their innocent mistakes.

Five Caveats

First Caveat

Path Finder will not show you how to awaken. This book is primarily meant to help you to recognize when you have been awakened, and how to take appropriate action. Once you have been awakened, or if you are now awakened, read the following chapters to learn how to maintain your awakened state, or find a compatible guide or guru to assist you on your path. This book may be used secondarily as a reference.

Second Caveat

Language and unfounded belief kept you asleep. They will not awaken you. Once you have been awakened though, language will be necessary to develop the principles you choose to live by, and once your principles are in place, language may be used to reference your heart's desire. Remember though, language can provide only a description of reality, and emotional states. More about this later…

Third Caveat

While principles are just another construct of language, they serve one useful purpose and that is as a protectant. The principles you develop are meant to keep you out of harm's way when interacting with other humans. Your principles will also keep you from losing your connection to your awakening. Your principles are your armor. Once you have committed to your principles, your life becomes much easier. You will lose fears. You will lose insecurities. You will be able to take meaningful action.

Fourth Caveat

You have already had many awakenings in your life, but you may not have been able to take advantage of them. Perhaps, you have just had an awakening, and you are now ready to act. If not, be at the ready when another such a moment arises, or when you choose to allow such a moment to arise, and then dive head first into what it has to teach you.

Fifth Caveat

Path Finder is directed at your intuitive, global thinking mind. Trust your intuitive mind. Listen for it. Your intuitive mind is your new best friend. The same applies to your heart.

"There are only two ways to live your life. One is as though nothing is a miracle. The other is as though everything is a miracle."

~ Albert Einstein

Triggers

"Triggers are like little psychic explosions that crash through avoidance and bring the dissociated, avoided trauma suddenly, unexpectedly, back into consciousness."

~ Carolyn Spring

Triggering Events

There are many triggers that can lead to a drastic shift in your world view, or your ability to be alive in the moment and to act on, and outside of, your unawakened state. This can happen spontaneously, and it can happen under guidance using formal practices and meditations.

Spontaneous, fortuitous, or what I like to call solo awakenings allow awareness shifts, usually following a change in your connection to the past, or an event that cannot be reconciled by your old beliefs or preconceptions. Without the anchor of interlocking beliefs, or being unable to act based past experience, you may able to enter the present, even if only momentarily.

Guided awakenings can be found through various techniques that redirect one away from the beliefs accumulated over a lifetime or redirect you to new beliefs. An example of this is the Alcoholics Anonymous program. More powerful still are practices or guidance that frees you from belief entirely.

It matters little how you came to be awakened. Solo awakenings are often beyond our conscious control, which is why they happen. As such, you may not have any support in maintaining your awakening. Path Finder is meant to support solo awakeners to find their path following an awakening. If those of you who have awakened through a guided awakening find this information useful as an adjunct to your practices, then I am grateful.

The advantage of guided awakenings is that you may have supports to guide you before and after your awakening. The disadvantage of guided awakenings is that the person or group offering the guidance, may help you let go of one or all your beliefs, only to replace them with new beliefs. Please be cautious of any system that does not provide ongoing support, or that introduces new *"better"* beliefs. This book is designed to help those choosing a guided awakening, as well as solo awakeners, to separate the *"wheat from the chaff,"* of these systems, and to also help find the path that calls you once you have awakened. However you awaken, whether solo or guided, a structure that includes principles and practices is needed to maintain your awakening.

Common Triggers

Awakenings are be triggered by many things. The following are some the more common ones. Some awakenings are more beneficial than others, but each has the possibility of bringing the awakened to a deeper understanding and connection in the moment, with the exception of those that awaken hate or revenge.

- You might have been awakened to a calamity such as COVID-19.
- You might have been awakened to formal guided meditation and practices.
- You might have been awakened to informal unguided meditation and practices.
- You might have been awakened to a shift from one belief to a new one.
- You might have been awakened to a realization of an hitherto unrecognized obstacle in your life.
- You might have been awakened to a realization that the path you are on might have been come to it's end.

- You might have been awakened to a shift of consciousness where you became aware of information that was unremembered, or suppressed, and is now available.
- You might have been awakened to a joyous or traumatic event.
- You might have been awakened by stepping outside your current worldview to see the world with "new eyes."
- You might have been awakened to a guided transformational practice.

If you have completely let go of belief, your awakening may allow you to become enlightened as described in Buddhist, Christian and Sufi esoteric traditions. The highest form of awakening is, when enlightened, to not just to be "in the moment," free of constraints and attachments, but to then to take action to positively impact the world. Not just letting go of beliefs and attachments to a world view, but to becoming an avatar to serve the further awakening of humankind, directly interceding in the asleep world, as a lucid dreamer in humanities' dream. Those so enlightened may then provide clarity, and serve as exemplars, or guides in humanity's search for balance, and to address the side-effects of human behaviour such as COVID-19.

Awakenings Through Joy or Trauma

"We need limitations and temptations to open our inner selves, dispel our ignorance, tear off disguises, throw down old idols, and destroy false standards. Only by such rude awakenings can we be led to dwell in a place where we are less cramped, less hindered by the ever-insistent External. Only then do we discover a new capacity and appreciation of goodness and beauty and truth."

~ Helen Keller

Many of us have experienced a profound shift in our perceptions relating to joyous moments or from traumas in our lives. These events can have a profound impact in awakening one to greater service, as is the case for many getting married, or undergoing childbirth. They can also trigger the opposite when loss is associated.

Tread carefully with traumatic awakenings. Get support if you need help. Get counseling if you need understanding. Surround yourself with loved ones, if possible. Do whatever you need to do to ease the pain you are experiencing, and to allow the pain to pass through you. Traumas can be as powerful as any belief that fails you. For those who assist you, the trauma may bring you closer together, making you better able to deal with the aftermath. Hearts serving hearts. Whether you have love and support, or if you are going it alone, traumas, rather than sinking you, may lead to awakening you to a life of purpose and caring, because traumas are often the opening of a door, a message that your life needs to change. If that is the case, this book is meant for you.

Examples of Joyous Awakenings
- Childbirth
- Cure or recovery from a disease
- Falling in love or marriage
- A new job or promotion
- Voluntary emigration
- A windfall

Examples of Traumatic Awakenings
Community, Regional, or World Events
- Epidemics and Pandemics
- War
- Revolution
- Famine
- Mass emigrations
- Earthquakes and natural events
- Political and economic events
- Local disasters, such as fires, building collapses, mine cave-ins, mass shootings, etc.

Personal Events
- Disease
- Mental Breakdown
- Divorce
- Incarceration
- Destitution
- Forced immigration
- Subjugation
- Starvation
- Injury or incapacitation
- Loss of a loved one
- Loss of work

True Awakenings

A true awakening is based on the releasing attachment to unfounded belief. A true awakening allows you to:
- Love without attachment
- Witness pain and suffering without attachment
- Free yourself from anger, hate, and rage
- See the world without filters
- Be a witness to love
- Be free to act without limits

Who Can I Trust?
- Trust those without belief.
- Trust those without motive.
- Trust those with nothing to gain.
- Trust those called by love, compassion and service.
- Trust those leading lives of selfless service.
- Trust those who speak from the heart, whose only message is love.
- Above all, trust *your* heart. Your heart is directly connected to your intuition, and your intuition is very good at detecting inauthenticity.

Dark Awakenings

Beware the lure of dark awakenings. Awakenings that seek revenge on an uncaring world. Awakenings that have hate at their core. Awakening founded in anger, hate and fear are to be avoided at all costs.

Dark Awakenings are easy to see by one outside the awakening, Not so easy when anger and rage is within you. Better to go back to sleep than to introduce the world to new ways to hate. Extreme care must also be taken to avoid taking on a new set of unfounded beliefs, or the recycling of old beliefs. If a belief has not served humankind and our animal cousins for ten thousand years, it is probably not going to work now.

Examples of Dark Awakenings
- Awakenings where a new set of beliefs have fear or hate at their core
- Awakenings where anger becomes hate
- Awakenings where hate becomes violence
- Awakenings where one bullied becomes the bully
- Awakenings where one bullied seeks revenge
- Awakenings where one disenfranchised seeks revenge
- Awakenings where *true believers* act out dogmatic fantasies
- Awakenings where proselytizers and religious leaders preach monetary gain and wealth
- Awakenings where generals seek war
- Awakenings where leaders seek conquest
- Awakenings where economies fail the poorest and weakest
- Awakenings where government policies denigrate those most in need
- Awakenings where enemies are posed to hide lies
- Awakenings where love is unfelt
- Awakenings where pain and suffering are unfelt

Who Should I Distrust
- Distrust governments that dismiss the needs of its citizens
- Distrust governments that do not act decisively and thoroughly to care for *all* of its citizens' health and wellbeing.

- Distrust governments that pose enemies rather that redressing the harm of their choices.
- Distrust governments that do not have equality and fairness as its highest principles.
- Distrust governments that imprisons those of conscience, or represses open discourse.
- Distrust politicians seeking favor from wealthy patrons.
- Distrust politicians who espouse hate and fear.
- Distrust *all* those who espouse hate and fear, or who make enemies of the downtrodden.
- Distrust those who denigrate other people, or low classes, or races, or orientations, or countries.
- Distrust the motives of billionaires, or those in service to billionaires.
- Distrust corporations where you are the product.
- Distrust religions where self-serving preachers propound gaining riches or fame.
- Distrust those who preach unfounded belief.
- Distrust economic systems of perpetual growth.
- Distrust those espousing inequality or separation.
- Distrust social media, and the motives of social media companies.
- Distrust generals, admirals and builders of weaponry.
- Distrust the enforcers and guardians of the status quo.

"Be the change you want to see in the World"
　　　　　　　　　　　　　　　　　~ Mahatma Gandhi

Who Would I Be?

Who would I be, and what would I do, if I could be the person I was before my persona began to form when I was born?

What could I accomplish if I ignored all the likes and dislikes of others in the world, and only followed my heart, my intuition, and my principles?

What would happen if I gave up the "need" to be liked or cared for?

What would happen if I stopped listening to my likes, dislikes and beliefs, and instead made my decisions solely by trusting my heart, my principles and my commitment to leaving the world a better place than I found it?

What would happen if I did not judge myself?

Would that require that I be true to myself?

What would happen if I listened to others without judgment?

Would that require that I see myself in the other person?

What would happen if I committed to always telling the truth, to always having complete integrity and to always seeking the highest good in all my choices?

Would a path be opened for me?

What would happen if I always noticed the details of the world, without judgment, just noticing, just observing, not thinking, just being?

Would the world seem a better place?

What would happen if I did not speak, unless I had something profound or revealing to say that clearly reflected my true nature?

What if truth and lies were subjective to the degree that I deny what my heart and intuition tells me?

What would happen If all the beliefs I use to define myself were not true or untrue, but only signposts on my path?

What would happen if I discarded my beliefs about myself and about others, even though my entire life has been devoted to keeping them polished to a high sheen?

What if there was no good and no bad within me, only love and compassion?

What if a thousand peers said I must look like them, must be like them, must think like them, must obey their consensus of beliefs in all matters and I said no?

Would I find truth within myself?

Would people who made the same choice as I, find me?

And who would I be if I became only my heart?

Then, who would I be?

CHAPTER THREE
Principles

"There will come a time when you believe everything is finished. That will be the beginning."

~ Louis L'Amour

Unfounded Belief

Asleep

If you have gotten this far. I will assume that you have had at least one awakening moment, or that an awakening is near. Your task is now to embed and strengthen your awakening, to protect it, and to put it to good use.

When I first awoke I realized that I had been asleep, and that those around me were asleep as well. I discovered over the next few years that what keeps us asleep more than anything else is belief. Especially unfounded belief. Acts of faith. Beliefs in gods and devils. Beliefs in myths. Beliefs in all that is unfounded or unknowable. The dramas people create out of beliefs, to paraphrase Shakespeare, *"told by idiots, full of sound and fury, signifying nothing."* We sleep because we believe in, and live inside worlds that are created while we are unconscious.

Belief and Religious Teachings

"I think of the Bible as an unauthorized biography," I think that the disciples were all trying to vie for their personal time that they spent around Jesus."

~ John Prine

Beliefs over time become an addiction, but the addiction to belief is not as powerful as the alcoholic's or drug user's addiction. After all, beliefs are just words. Once you have had an awakening though, you may have trouble letting go of disempowering religious or other beliefs. Often they hold their sway due to dogmatic teachings embedded in your mind when you were young. Letting go those dogmatic teachings will release the hold of the belief.

The easiest way to release religious or other dogmatic belief is to deliberately ignore all the dogma of a belief system or of a religion, and focus only on what the original teacher said.

The dogmatic teachings by many religions, and other pseudo-religious systems frequently diminishes or ignores the underlying values of the original teaching. Focus only on what the original teacher or master said, and whether the message is to love or to hate. If it is to hate, or seeks monetary prosperity, or if it poses enemies, or justifies wars, ignore it all. If the message is love, then view the teachings as a set of moral guidelines, or principles for you to follow. *e.g. Do unto others...* For example, when Jesus said, *"turn the other cheek,"* but the preacher* says, *"an eye for an eye,"* you may be sure that the preacher is not preaching the words of Jesus. If a Buddhist sect includes beliefs in their dogma, you might look elsewhere. Buddha taught his followers to let go of *all* belief. Nothing added. If a preacher of good heart follows the teachings of the original master, in words *and* deeds, listen to, and add their words to your spiritual code, if they align with your principles.

*Note: Preacher is shorthand for a priest, minister, rabbi, imam, monk, shaman, guru, spiritual guide, etc.

Letting go belief

So, what does all this talk of belief and dogma have to do with your path and the principles you will need to maintain it? Just this. If you are attached to your beliefs, your first action is not an exploration of a new belief. For the time being, first on your to-do list is to develop the principles you will live by, and to begin letting go of the beliefs controlling your every waking moment.

Your awakening will suffice to keep some, or all of your beliefs at bay, as it may be belief's failure that caused your awakening. For other beliefs you will need to research alternative ways of thinking not based on belief. To let go the rest you might be ready to begin meditating, or following a practice. You might start by taking nature walks and observations, or gardening with intention. Write poetry, start a journal, join a meditation group or whatever practice that calls your heart. These activities will also help to distract your linear mind and the control it has over you, and to call forth your intuitive mind and heart. Begin your meditations and practices as soon after your awakening as possible. For more on this, see Chapter Five.

I started out by using walking meditation, driving meditation, meditative writing, lucid dreaming and the doing of meditative tasks. Over time that evolved into a larger meditation. Meditation and practices are not an end in themselves though. They are tools. What unfolds from meditation and practices is a reduction in linear thinking, and greater access to intuition and your heart. You are literally switching control from the left side of your brain to the right. Those activities will also help you to relax, and allow you to start making connections.

They help bring out conscious thinking, greater awareness of self and most importantly, they will assist you to be aware of beliefs as they arise.

Awakening and recognizing the beliefs that held you hostage puts you on a path to rediscovering your true nature. What comes next is the examination and development of principles you wish to live by, free from belief. Without the crutch of belief, you can start to develop your own internalized principles for living your life as a meditation, and retraining your innate intuition to recognize and ignore unfounded belief.

What *are* Principles?

"Principles are not for the times when there is no temptation: they are for such moments as this, when body and soul rise in mutiny against their rigor... If at my convenience I might break them, what would be their worth?"

~ Charlotte Brontë, Jane Eyre

Principles
Dictionary definition:

An accepted or professed rule of action or conduct: a person of good moral principles; a fundamental, primary, or general law or truth from which others are derived: the principles of modern physics: a fundamental doctrine or tenet; a distinctive ruling opinion: the principles of the Stoics.

Path Finder definition:

Principles are a way to ensure *"right"* action as well as a way to trigger ethical actions, without being attached to a belief, or beliefs that require a given outcome, or that can be thwarted by circumstance. A principle might be, I will take care of my family without reservation, or I will seek to do good in the world, or I will be kind to animals wherever I find them, or I will forgive myself my failures so that I may do good in the world. The Path Finder definition of a principle does not include benefit to yourself, but does include benefit to a greater purpose. With a principle, the sky's the limit, and a principle has unlimited ways to be expressed. Principles are not attached to specific actions or outcomes. Principles are attached to intention and focus. Principles allow us to live by our wits, to listen to our own inner voice, without the chatter of doubt. We can fail in our attempts to do good, but giving up our principles is not a choice, rather we must find new ways to express them.

What is Good and Right Action?

"The most important consideration is not the right action in itself but a right inward state out of which right action will arise. Given the right inward state, right action is inevitable."

~ Howard Brinton

For an unawakened person good, and right action are difficult to explain. The unawakened live inside the crosstalk of beliefs, myths and dogma, and can have little understanding, control or recognition of good and right action, except through the clouded lens of contradictory beliefs. For the awakened, good is an alignment between your intuitive mind, your heart, your chosen principles, and your intention.

To awaken, is to turn your life over to the wisdom of your intuitive mind and heart. Your principles are where you determine what good is. Good must be be clearly stated in your principle. e.g. "I will love my neighbor, without reservation." When you devise your principles, keep this in mind. Your principles work most powerfully when belief or specific actions are not included. My experience tells me, for example, that you do not have to believe in a god to be an honorable loving person. You do not have to believe anything to be a loving person. All that is required is that you *are* a loving person. Belief will not help you to maintain your self-awareness. If you choose a religious teaching, ignore any dogma and only focus on the underlying message of love. Let that be what guides you. The rest is up to you and your intuitive mind.

Maintaining Your Awakening

"Bliss is to be in action without expectation."

~ Abhijit Naskar

To maintain your awakening, start with your principles. Not only do they serve as protectants from the asleep world, but they also offer protection from your linear mind's impulses and desire for dominance. This may not be easy at first.

The two biggest obstacles are old habits and a life lived without integrity. The first principle you will need is one that states your commitment to maintaining your awakening, and the following of your principles one hundred percent of the time. That first principle will be the filter that all your other principles and all you subsequent action will be guided by. When you have an awakening moment, you will also be re-opening pathways to your intuitive mind. Your intuitive mind may well become fully functional following your awakening. If it didn't, it would be difficult to come up with any effective principles. It is possible that you will not consciously make that decision, but your intuitive mind will know why it is so important, and keep trying to show you the way. If that is the case, listen fully.

If your intuitive mind has been drowning under the weight of your myriad belief dreams, it can to life immediately upon your awakening. Perhaps, or I should say probably, your intuitive mind is the cause of your awakening, and it had just gotten tired of waiting for you to figure it out. You don not have to examine what instigated your awakening. You will be so busy being grateful that it had given you a second chance in my life, that you might forgot to ask.

The principles you first devise will be the basis for who you are to become, and what you are to do. When you adhere to your principles *all* of the time something miraculous takes place. First, you find that you have very few choices, and that those choice are clear. Second, as your intuitive mind takes over, it will continue to seek new avenues for you to do good and to find fulfillment. That is the way it works.

When you have one hundred percent integrity, your intuitive mind knows it. When you chose a life of integrity, your intuitive mind knows it. When you determine the principles your will live by, your intuitive mind knows it. When you chose to be a *"lover"* in the Sufi sense, your intuitive mind knows it. Your intuitive mind is eager to serve you. This could be your greatest revelation upon awakening.

Doing good makes you good. Being good makes you do good. It is not about choice anymore. Integrity releases you from choice, but not from a great diversity of possible actions. In fact, the actions you can take are not only more varied, but they are vastly more fulfilling. You find yourself giving things away that you once thought precious. Your voice now speaks with kindness. You notice the suffering of others. Your acts become expressions of love. Love becomes *you*.

Second, your intuitive mind loves to assist you on your one hundred percent path. Loves it! The intuitive mind's purpose becomes the fulfilling of all of your principles by recognizing moments where you can do good, and then encourages you to do good. Your intuitive mind eagerly spots *good* in a crowded room, and nudges you forward to action. This is called *"Right Action."* It is beyond *belief*. You are following your principles as guided by your intuitive mind and your heart.

For the awakened person there is no good or bad, except in the present moment, and in that moment great things are possible, including fundamental shifts in the direction we, and those around us, may take.

Being in the World, Not of the World

To be awakened also allows you to be *"In the world, not of the world."* The term "be in the world, not of the world" can be found in Jewish, Christian, Muslim, Sufi, and Buddhist teachings. Buddhism describes *Maya* as illusion, unreality, and deception among other things, and *Maya* is commonly used to convey being *"of the world,"* trapped by illusion. To be *"in the world, not of the world,"* is to not be influenced or attached to the world of illusion and beliefs. At a higher level, to *"be in the world"* makes it possible to act upon the world, for the good of humankind, and the Earth, with both clarity and purpose, and without attachment to ego or outcomes. The terms "being in the world", "being in the moment", "being present", and "being here now" all refer to the state of grace attained when we let go of belief and attachment.

"Love cannot exist when there is a self. Love is boundless. It is selfless, and therefore it exists beyond the confines and limitations of the self. Love is much more than a word: It is an immeasurable force that only exists when there is no division, when one is whole."
~ Nicholas Blewett, Freedom From the Self

Your Principles
Guidelines

"According to Buddhism, compassion is an aspiration, a state of mind, wanting others to be free from suffering. It's not passive— it's not empathy alone— but rather an empathetic altruism that actively strives to free others from suffering. Genuine compassion must have both wisdom and loving kindness. That is to say, one must understand the nature of the suffering from which we wish to free others (this is wisdom), and one must experience deep intimacy and empathy with other sentient beings (this is loving kindness)."

~ Dalai Lama

Avoid principles that make you feel good or feel bad, hopeful or not hopeful, loving or hateful, believing or disbelieving. Instead focus on principles that ensure your awakening and that will aid in the maintenance of the path you choose to follow.

The Purpose of Principles
- Principles are protectants, meant to further your awakening, both internally and externally.
- Principles are meant to embed your awakening.
- Principles are meant to move you forward.
- Principles are meant to support the path you choose.

Your principles may assist you in letting go beliefs and judgment. So choose wisely, and listen to your heart and to your intuitive mind. As you let go reliance on belief, your principled intuition will take over, and you will find that the decisions you now make will come more easily, be more effective and be more satisfying.

A Word to the Wise

Choosing the principles for the path you choose can be complicated. You may start out with principles that are few and narrowly focused as I initially did. Down the road you may find those principles inadequate, again, as I did. Rather than keep adding principles as your life evolves, it might be better to include more universal principles that will encompasses those changes. For example, instead of having a principle that says, *"I will be kind to children,"* you might say, *"I will be kind to all humans,"* or even more encompassing, *"I will be kind and compassionate to all of Earth's children."* At the least, leave room for your principle to grow as you grow. At best, your principles will raise you beyond what you may now think possible.

100% Principles — A Caution

When you choose the principle that states *"I will honor my principles, without fail, one hundred percent of the time,"* be absolutely sure you have let go of *all* unfounded beliefs. If your linear mind is still entangled in belief, you will likely fail to uphold this vital principle. Your long-held beliefs will try to trip you up, and prove to you that they were right all along. They will try to belittle you and shame you with guilt if you fail. Your remaining beliefs are like demons that *must* be cast out. Do *not* allow yourself to be tricked. Let go *all* your beliefs, especially unfounded ones. Then you can completely give over your life to this principle and keeping your awakening alive, as well as strengthening your intuitive mind. This principle is your awakening's primary protectant. Value it above all else.

First Principles
Protectants

"I think a spiritual journey is not so much a journey of discovery. It's a journey of recovery. It's a journey of uncovering your own inner nature. It's already there."

~ Billy Corgan

Upon awakening, you will realize that you need some protection from old beliefs, old habit, selfish impulses and the ephemeral comfort they offer, as well as old acquaintances who might resist the change you have undergone.

When you have an awakening moment, you are also re-opening pathways to your intuitive mind, the part of your mind where consciousness resides. Your intuitive mind never left you, and has tried to warn you of danger and the taking of wrong paths. Your *conscience*, perhaps a small part of the intuitive mind's awareness, was all your beliefs begrudgingly might have allowed you to see. For many, beliefs do not allow even that sliver of the intuitive mind to appear. We think we can ignore its cautions, as we pursue the latest selfish impulse, and mostly we do not listen. That is the power that belief has over us. Our intuitive mind is never completely suppressed by the weight of our beliefs though, and when we awaken, our intuitive mind becomes fully available, if we allow it. It becomes critical, if we wish to keep the intuitive minds at the fore, to take some steps to guard its availability. This starts with our principles. Not only do they serve as protectants from the asleep world's allure, but they also offer protection from your linear mind's desire for dominance. This may not be easy at first. The biggest obstacles are old beliefs, old habits and a life lived without integrity.

So, the first principle you need is one that states your commitment to maintaining your awakening, and that you will follow your principles, one hundred percent of the time. This first principle will be the filter that all your other principles and your subsequent action will be guided by. Your intuitive mind, without the fetters of belief, will know why it was so important, and in your moment of awakening will step forward and take charge, if you allow it..

Principles are not beliefs. They are simply conscious choices you make about how you will act from this moment forward. That is why you have to remain aware of them at all times and use them to filter all your actions. One of the unintended consequences to adhering to your principles is finding how simple it is to be honorable, to always tell the truth. The principles will ripple through all your thoughts, and became the guideposts for all of your actions. It soon became very difficult to do any activity that betrayed the promises you make to yourself, but not resisting the mandates of your principles greatly helps.

These are principles that might get you started:

I will honor my principles without fail one hundred percent of the time.
I will hold my principles higher that any view or belief.
I will not bow to impulses contrary to my principles.
I will do my best, without reservation.
I will give and accept love unconditionally.
I will do nothing I would fear admitting to another.
I will be kind and compassionate.
I will trust my heart to guide me.

The following are principles you may also find useful:

I will love unconditionally.

I will assume nothing.

I will abandon unfounded belief and views when proven false.

I will be honest to myself and to others.

I will not lie, cheat or steal.

I will correct wrongs I have done, and make them right.

I will not turn away from suffering.

I will act without selfish intent.

I will disparage no one.

I will not judge the intentions of others.

I will not gossip or disparage others.

I will not judge others, nor their intentions.

I will assume nothing.

I will love all of Earth's creatures.

I will be awake to the life that surrounds me.

I will be awake to others on the path with me.

"When you commit to 100% integrity, the need for affirmations becomes unnecessary. A simple to do list will suffice. If you still enjoy saying affirmations, start your statements with 'I will...'"
~ Johnny Peaceseed, *Momentary Memoirs*

Loving and Being of Service

To be most effective, your principles must include a commitment to being a loving person and should reflect a commitment of service to others. Your awakening allows you to think big, and by being loving and of service to others, doubt and self-involvement will dissipate. By letting go of these anchors to the past, your life gains new freedom and unlimited possibilities.

You might ask, why do I have to love, when there is so much hateful behavior in the world? The answer is certainly not so you will get to heaven, as lovely as that story sounds. It is because, by loving, you protect yourself from belief, and second, in truly loving, you ask nothing for yourself. This is absolutely critical, because one who surrenders to love can have no expectation, and it is only without expectation, that one can truly witness the world, and thus be present to it. The same cannot be said about hate, and gratefully so.

Suggestions for Principles

If any of the Sample Principles above resonate with you, feel free to use them, and add any of your own principles that will further your heart's call. You will want to print a copy, or copies of your principles to post where you can see them every day. This is part of the embedding process. Put them on your to-do list, on your calendar, in your diary and wherever else you think will be useful. Memorize them. Every decision you make from this point forward will be in accordance with how you have chosen to become.

Add new principles as needed, but do not waiver in your commitment, and do not remove the prime principle to act with integrity 100% of the time. The power of your awakening flows through your principles, then into your practices and on to your path where your intention will create actions that will impact the world. This will help you maintain focus on your path, and protect your awakening. Once again, it is important to remember that these are promises to yourself and they require one hundred percent willing compliance to become embedded. The one hundred percent part is most important as you explore your awakened self. If, at a later date, you choose to change, delete or add new principles that will further drive your awakening, do not hesitate. You are perfecting you, for you, but you are also perfecting yourself that you may better serve the humanity and the Earth.

Your Principles

Now, without any pressure, write down the principles you wish to live by. Take your time. Reflect. Listen to your heart. You can add or change them later, if you so desire. Look, I have filled in the first one for you:

I Choose to Live My Life By These Principles:

1. I will honor my principles 100% of the time.
2. I will
3. I will
4. I will
5. I will
6. I will
7. I will
8. I will
9. I will
10. I will

Now Remind Yourself

Go to your electronic calendar and create a new repeating event that will appear every morning at the same time, or several times per day. Title the event *Awaken*. You are done, your calendar is now ready to serve you. If *Awaken* is too loud, choose something else such as *Honor my principles*, or whatever might be useful to you. These daily, or frequent repetitions might help you maintain alertness to your principles and your practices.

CHAPTER FOUR
Practices

"Self-respect is the root of discipline: The sense of dignity grows with the ability to say no to oneself."

~ *Abraham Joshua Heschel*

Definitions

Practices
Definition of Practices
To perform or work at repeatedly so as to become proficient

Systematic exercise for proficiency

Meditation
Definition of Meditation
To engage in mental exercise (such as concentration on one's breathing or repetition of a mantra) for the purpose of reaching a heightened level of spiritual awareness

Mindfulness
Definition of Mindfulness
The practice of maintaining a nonjudgmental state of heightened or complete awareness of one's thoughts, emotions, or experiences on a moment-to-moment basis

Taking Control
Taking Control of Your Awakening
You will need to find practices to provide consistency and a structure that will help you maintain your awakened state. The discipline that is needed to maintain a meditation is as vital as the meditation itself. This is a good example why it is so useful to work with a guide or guru. Thousands of years of tradition can smooth the rough spots and correct weaknesses in a practice.

We will now examine the disciplines, meditations, or mindfulness techniques you might use to maintain your awakening. The rest is reasonably easy.

First, start by trying out different meditations, mantras, mindfulness or other techniques to see which are most effective for you. Learn all you can about the techniques and theory, and pros and cons. Keep looking at as many ways to maintain wakefulness as you can. *Look as if your life depended on it!*

As you practice, keep your principles at the fore. Your principles, to become embedded, will need to be repeated, until they become second nature.

You might find yourself gravitating to one practice or another, or with a teacher you might connect with. Be sure you are not gravitating to that person because of an attraction to the person teaching it. You do not want to be like that person, at all. Your goal is to be you, not a reflection of someone else. That is your focus. Just focus on the practice and see if it helps with the embedding of your principles.

Some practices will be difficult, but that is not an excuse to look elsewhere. Instead look at the results that adherents achieve, before you decide to accept or reject it, but do not listen to the advice of adherents, unless you can clearly see how it facilitated the opening of their consciousness.

Avoid any practice that demands that you change your beliefs for new ones. Remember, you are seeking freedom from belief. Programs that are money driven should be looked upon with suspicion, until you are sure of their underlying intention.

Once you have cleared from your mind the shackles of unfounded belief your reawakened intuitive mind, and your heart, will be able to effectively guide you on your path.

Acting on Your Practices

Determine how much time you can devote to your practices. Then, adhere to your practices *"religiously."* Unfettered intention and follow through are all that matters. Jettison any practice that you will not stay committed to, or at least ask yourself why you are not following the practice, and make the corrections that will get you back on track. Continue your practice if you are getting the result you are after, and do not give one up if you do not see results immediately. You might try some practices that you are uncomfortable with, but the discomfort could be a sign that they might just what you need. Again, trust your unfettered intuition and your heart.

The following are a sampling of meditations or practices you might consider both before and after your awakening. None of these lists are close to complete. If you feel pulled by one, that is a good first step. Pursue it.

Guided Meditations and Practices to induce or maintain an awakening

Christian and Muslim
- Prayer, Being reborn (Christian), Rituals

Buddhist
- Zen Koans, Mantras, Rituals

Sufi
- Dance, Prayer, Rituals

Individual Movement
- Yoga, Tai Chi, Dance

Recovery and treatment programs
- Psychiatrists, Counselors, Therapists

Empowerment Programs
- Rebirthing, Landmark, Lifespring, Guided Retreats, etc.

Rituals – Formal and Informal
- Breathing, Mantras, Prayer, Chanting, Reiki

Practices where spontaneous or solo awakenings might be maintained

Meditations
- Mindfulness, Breathing, Prayer, Mantras, Chanting, Stillness, Reiki

Movement
- Yoga, Tai Chi, Dance

Individual Practices

Rituals – Informal
- Breathing, Walking, Running, Driving, Swimming, Gardening, Childcare, Eldercare, Daily interactions, Intimacy, etc.

Every Moment is a Meditation
(For Advanced Practitioners)

Sleeping is a meditation.
Dreams are a meditation.
Releasing beliefs is a meditation.
Walking is a meditation.
Driving is a meditation.
Writing is a meditation.
Every communication is a meditation.
Dish washing is a meditation.
Laundry day is a meditation.
Gardening is a meditation.
Every chore is a meditation.
Every bodily function is a meditation.
Love is a meditation.
Kindness is a meditation.
Every waking moment is a meditation.
Every sleeping moment is a meditation.
Every moment is a meditation.

When everything is a meditation or a mindfulness practice, it is very easy to see whether you are in, or out of the moment. When the practice becomes everything you do, you will maintain your principles, maintain your intentions, and take action

CHAPTER FIVE
Path Finder

"Awakening without purpose is like a fish swimming without water, or a bird flying without air. A message without a medium."

~ Johnny Peaceseed, Momentary Memoirs

Flying Solo
Purpose

"The purpose of life is a life of purpose."

~ Robert Byrne

It took me many years of flying solo to realize that my awakening required that I put my gift into action, to be of service, to look beyond my own personal desires. One of the advantages to flying solo is that you can be more closely aligned to your heart's desires. The downside, as was the case with me, is that you might not be able to see the bigger picture, or have the knowledge to put your awakening into effective action. I eventually figured this out, but not without many trials and some tribulation. If you do not feel comfortable on the solo journey, I suggest that you take the time to find a guide or guru who will help to keep you on your path. The path I chose was needlessly arduous, with many false starts. However, if you are wiser than I, perhaps it will not take you as long. Just keep a belief free guide or guru in mind if you falter, or lose your way.

The world needs those awakened. There are some who think that, without the awakened, the world would be in a far worse predicament. I am among those. Can you imagine a world where turning the other cheek was not an option? Can you imagine a world without non-violent protests of injustice? Can you imagine if women had not marched for equal rights over a century ago. If labor unions had not stood up to corporations? A world without Mahatma Gandhi and all those he inspired, or Simon Bolivar and Che Guevara, or Emma Goldman, or Rosa Parks? These exemplars resisted the dominant paradigm of repressive and suppressive belief. They imagined a better world, and against all odds, helped bring real change.

The world needs your wisdom, your expertise, your awakened heart. Since we cannot rely on leaders who do not lead, and followers who no longer follow, it is up to those awake who are willing to act, and to step into the fray. Your task is to find that which calls you most fervently. You may be required to let go the safety net of a steady job, or a steady life, to seek your true calling. If you are responsible for the wellbeing of others, you will have to act in their interest as well. If you are persistent, you may be able to do both at once.

If you work for any polluting or extractive corporation, you might consider changing jobs, or perhaps you could work inside the corporation to change its mission, or be a whistleblower, if the place you work lacks ethical standards. If you are a stockholder in a company, demand accountability and a plan to drastically reduce emissions. If you work for an oil company or an investment bank, or a munitions manufacturer, your choices will be easy. Perhaps some of you will run for office. Others will become organizers.

Think what a sixteen year old girl was able to accomplish when she was called. Now, that you are the one who is called it is time to ask what you are called to do? If something in your life breaks your heart, perhaps it is your path calling out to you. If today's events bring tears to your eyes, perhaps those tears are calling you to action. If you witness injustice, or cruelty, or hate, your heart may guide you. Your heart know all that is of true import. When your heart calls you, and when you answer your heart's call, you are absolved of all of your previous mistakes, and forgiven where you have failed. You are redeemed by your calling, by your path and the purpose you give your life to.

There is a beauty and symmetry to being of service, and being selfless in that service. If you have family or a group you live with, you will perhaps need to find work that sustains your family or group. If that is the case, choose well your work. You might also devote your time outside of work to volunteering your services to aid an environmental effort or other important cause. The work best suited to one awakened does not usually require spending time with organizations doing harm to the earth. Please choose wisely.

Who Will Be Called
Past Leaders Will Not Be Called
Past leaders will not be the new leaders. We cannot afford to make the same mistakes again. The worst of the old leaders had some or all of these traits:

- They had great egos and narcissistic personalities.
- They harbored great insecurities.
- They had rigid belief systems.
- They sought self-aggrandizement and personal gain.
- They were duplicitous.
- They posed enemies.
- They had hate and fear at their core.

All of these traits are unacceptable in a leader from this point forward!

Today's New Leaders
The leaders we need for the transition of humanity away from belief and towards restoration must have the following traits:

- They are awakened and enlightened.
- They exemplify honesty and integrity in all that they do.
- They are free from attachment to dogma or belief.
- They are kind, loving and selfless.
- Their greatest impulse is to be of service.
- They are non-violent.

- They practice a discipline that keeps them in the moment.
- They have clear intentions.
- They are ready to take action.

These traits are found in great spiritual teachers and leaders in the past, such as Jesus Christ and The Buddha. If you yearn to be a leader and you are awakened, you will need to prepare for your calling by perfecting your principles and practices, opening yourself to love and service and freeing yourself from belief. When that is done, your intuitive mind and heart will guide you.

For Those Who Prefer to Follow

Powerful leaders are not powerful unless they have powerful followers. They will need help. They will need guidance, expertise and skills that you could provide. They will need help to bring your path to fruition.

Before you choose to follow a person called to leadership, please review this chapter. You need to be certain that they pass your intuitive mind's scrutiny.

Leaders for Tomorrow — Part One

"We need enlightenment, not just individually but collectively, to save the planet. We need to awaken ourselves. We need to practice mindfulness if we want to have a future, if we want to save ourselves and the planet."

~ Thich Nhat Hanh

The next generation of enlightened leaders will guide humanity away from its worst impulses. When they have been successful, humanity will be able to then change the course of childhood. We will be able to raise children who will never have to experience lives inside of belief and dogma. To be born, and to live free of attachment, will be a tremendous boon to how they see the world, and the actions they may take. These children will truly be the vanguard of a new age. And what leaders they will become!

Preparation to Find Your Path

"The cities, the roads, the countryside, the people I meet – they all begin to blur. I tell myself I am searching for something. But more and more, it feels like I am wandering, waiting for something to happen to me, something that will change everything, something that my whole life has been leading up to."
~ *Khaled Hosseini, And the Mountains Echoed*

Unbeliever

How do I find my Path? How best can I make a difference? These are questions that can only be answered by each individual. Your path, like everything else about you is unique to you. To find your path you must first be awakened. Otherwise, you will only be able to supplant one belief with another, and will not be able to maintain your awakening or to find your true calling. If you are awakened and have developed principles and practices to maintain your awakening, you now are ready to cleanse any remaining beliefs.

Until now, belief controlled most of your existence, so it might be difficult to bid some beliefs not related to your awakening adieu. One born to slavery, when their shackles are removed may feel adrift, for the same reason. A lifetime of bondage scars deeply. If you have been wounded, be kind to yourself. Forgive yourself. Forgive the choices you made. Forgive those who brought you harm. Forgive the human race, as it continues to slumbers. This includes your leaders, your bosses and all the bullies that you have suffered. They are no longer your nemeses.

You have no enemies now, and your old beliefs and any remaining anger will not further you on your newfound path. Love is that which you now serve. Love of the Earth, love of family, love for those who suffer. It is love that you now must hold most dear. You are becoming a bringer of change. You are now under the direction of your heart and your intuition.

Letting go each belief is freeing, but may leave you feeling unmoored. If that is so, then go slowly. Start by following a practice that will calm your mind and let you examine each belief carefully, without feeling you have something to lose. When a belief no longer holds you, release it, as you would release a bird caught in a snare, with the utmost care and kindness. Those beliefs were your closest friends. Thank them for all they taught you, but they are your friends no more. Your new best friends are your heart, your intuition, your principles and your new-found purpose. Love your new friends and let them help you find your way.

Preparing to Find Your Path

To start, make a list of all your concerns for your family, your community and the world at large. Some items on your list may be merged with others if you wish. The purpose of this list is to alert your intuitive mind to be ready to act. If the Spoken World, filled with belief and linear though processes, has been suppressing or denying your native intuition, you might find this difficult. Once you have your principles and practices in place, you can start quieting you linear mind's chattering for attention, and you can begin listening for to intuitive mind. Using your meditations and practices will help. Spending time in nature will help as well. The advantage you have, if recently awakened, is that you are now more capable of gaining access to your intuitive mind, as you keep releasing the remaining chains of belief. Keep focused, night and day, listening for your path. Your intuition and heart will be your guide in every decision and every choice you make.

Anything in conflict with your principles, or your intuition requires a thorough reexamination, or a halt to the activity you were about to undertake. If your principles come in conflict with any lingering beliefs you still cling to, let go those beliefs, rather than your principles, no matter how difficult that might be. You are breaking lifelong bonds. Those bonds may be former commitments, former friends, a former life. Let them go. You do not want to keep tripping over them. As you keep following your heart and intuition, your path becomes clearer. Your path will start to guide all your actions, and your every waking moment will start to be in service to your path.

The Direction of Your Path

If you wish to serve your heart but need an income, or if you want to work with others on established paths please see the section on avocations and vocations for some ideas. If you understand the requirements of the path calling you, or you are going to work with others in fulfilling a shared path, I offer a few suggestions:

- Research your path and examine any pitfalls you might encounter before beginning. Research how others addressed similar pitfalls and how they were overcome.
- Some paths may be part of a larger path, that might yield the change you seek, while furthering a greater good as well. An example might be your desire to help homeless children. If the engine that puts children on the street is poverty caused by income inequality, perhaps you might consider both as your path "to help two birds with one commitment."
- Put you heart into your path. Heart and intuition trump everything. Heart and intuition are now your guides.

- Before you speak to a potential ally, get your facts straight.
- Before you speak to one who could become an obstacle to your path empty yourself of fear, judgment and expectation. Treat them with the same respect that you would an ally and listen to what they say with your heart. You might find commonality, or even a new ally.
- When you speak, let your intuition and heart speak the words. Chit chat is no longer an ally. Words from your heart will be listened to, and will be more eloquent.
- Consider not using disempowering words. e.g. should and shouldn't, could and can't, would and won't, belief, believe, wish, hope, faith, pray, prayer and sports and combat terms, etc.
- Be in the moment when speaking and listening to others. Look them in the eye. Listen to what others have to say. You are in a dance when you speak with others. Enjoy the dance.

Seeking Others on the Same Path

Start with internet, library and telephone book searches for like-minded people and groups. Read local newspapers, and blogs relating to your path. If you wish, you may bypass the hive minds of Twitter and Facebook. You are not looking for people who think alike. You are looking for those who can think, free from likes and dislikes. Look up research efforts related to your path and see if any research has been done in your community. Post help wanted ads at local stores and markets, and maybe in your local newspaper. Be persistent. Do not give up easily. Think outside the box. Be innovative. Give your big brain a good workout, until it finds connections, even if it takes you to people or places you did not expect.

If you fail to find those you seek through the above means, do not leave your path, and do not become discouraged. You may have to generate the call to others to join your path. You may have to learn to do public speaking. You may have to post invites to meetings. You may have to take up writing or create a blog advocating your path's direction. Tell your friends and colleagues of your new calling. You might be surprised at who steps forward. As a final resort, you may still go it alone, as I initially did. The one great thing about going solo, is that there are no rules, Roberts or otherwise, only your heart and mind to create the path you will follow. Being on a solo path can lead to relationships, connections and allies far beyond what you might have thought possible.

Be open to all possibilities, but choose carefully. Traveling a false path predicated by self-interest, fear, or hate will lead nowhere. All you will learn is what not to do. When you begin it, your path is a blank slate, ready to be filled with all you dream of. As you develop it, your path will take shape, it become less malleable, more certain and clearer. Your choices become clearer as well. Leave the rest to your heart and intuition.

Work in Service to Others

You may find that serving others is very rewarding. If you need to work to sustain yourself and your family, look at which skills you have that might be transferable to work that moves the human race forward What skills would you need to acquire, or that you could learn at work? What work would be most fulfilling to you? Would you rather make a complete break from your previous work? Or is the work you do now transferable to your awakened life? After examining all the possibilities, you might try interning if you are not sure of work that would serve your path. A careful listening to your heart and intuition always helps.

Finding Your Path
Intention and Perfection

"Times are difficult globally; awakening is no longer a luxury or an ideal. It's becoming critical. We do not need to add more depression, more discouragement, or more anger to what's already here. It's becoming essential that we learn how to relate sanely with difficult times. The earth seems to be beseeching us to connect with joy and discover our innermost essence. This is the best way that we can benefit others."

~ Pema Chödrön

Intention

Dictionary Definition:
An aim that guides action.

Path Finder Definition:
Intention refers to those awakened and their quest to put into action their awakened moment. For those awake, an intention is not an action. Intention resides in our heart and intuition. Intention points to doing an action. It is fluid. If you were to say, *"I will serve good"* in all my actions, that is your intention. However you choose to serve good is dependent on the moment, the place, your intuition and your abilities. Thus, intention can have wildly divergent ways of being expressed. In contrast, commitment is an expression of your intention. For instance, you will commit to be at a certain place, at a certain time and perform a certain act. That is a commitment. A commitment is, like your word, a bond, that must honored. If, for some reason, you are not able to fulfill a commitment, you must take appropriate action to either re-commit to the action, redress your failure to act, or make a new commitment

to some equally high purpose within your intention's bounds. There are no free lunches with commitment, or it is not a commitment.

Awakened
Dictionary Definition:
To become conscious or aware of something, as in being awakened from a deep sleep, or as in a new generation awakening to the importance of political action.

Path Finder Definition:
Awakened refers to those who, through meditation and practices, or through an event in their life, either joyous or traumatic, were able to let go of old beliefs and habits, to see the world with *"new eyes,"* as in, a veil lifted, a profound personal realization, a release from a pattern of behavior, or a eureka moment of self-awareness.

The Paths Before Us
Our intentions direct us to do all in our power to confront and correct the harm we see in the world and its underlying causes. It is clear that humanity urgently needs to look at new ways of thinking to address all that needs redressing. The first step is to acknowledge the mistakes and failures of the near and distant past. The second step is to transfer our allegiance to enlightened leaders, or to be those enlightened leaders ourselves. The third step is to institute fundamental changes in how we connect with the natural world. The fourth step is to change the way we connect with each other.

We are in the midst of the greatest crises ever to have faced humanity. Our children's lives are at stake. Our families are at stake. Our communities are at stake. The Earth is at stake. This moment is also our greatest opportunity to evolve beyond our lives of unfounded belief. It is by our intentions, by our commitments and by our actions that we will determine humanity's fate and the fate of Mother Earth.

Perfect Yourself

Perfect yourself before seeking to help others. Before you try to convince others to join you on your path, you must have already made the transition to living the life you wish for others. Apologize to those you have harmed. Forgive those who have harmed you. Clean up your messes, and make the changes in your life that will maximize the likelihood of success on your path Train your self and seek verifiable knowledge to bolster tour understanding.

Train Your Intuition

Once you have cleared your mind of unfounded belief, it will be necessary to retrain your intuitive global thinking mind to recognize and use verifiable accurate information in your decision making, and to carefully assess the choices you will be making. Once you have *front-loaded* your mind with accurate data and determined how to will use it, your intuitive powers will expand greatly. One note about your intuitive mind though, is that while it can process a much greater amount of information that your linear mind, its calculations may not reveal the why's of the results it produces. That is why it is necessary for you to seek verifications of the accuracy of the data you provided. *Garbage in, garbage out.*

You Are Ready

When all that you do, and all that you say, and all of your actions are in alignment with your chosen path, you will be ready. When your intention and commitment to serve the furtherance of humankind's awakening manifests within you, and in those sharing the same path, you will all take action. You will be joined by countless others to sweep the old world order into the dustbin of history. You will all speak with clear hearts and clear minds. Humanity will see you, and they will hear you, and they will know the love in your hearts and they will trust your words, for you have nothing to hide, and nothing to fear.

Now is the Time

What are your principles? What are your intentions? What are your commitments? What action will you take? Is everyone ready?

Perfection

Hold a mirror up to your face. Look at the person looking back at you. Ignore the tiny flaws that might keep you from seeing perfection. Can you not see it? No? Take two steps back. Now? Twirl around three times and look again. Now? Wake up! Wake up! Look deeply into those eyes. There you are. There you were all along, you perfect human.

Perfection, like beauty, is not skin deep. Perfection, and beauty, emanates from our hearts. Any other manifestation of perfection, or beauty, is irrelevant. Superficial. A trap that keeps us in our beliefs. Jesus Christ was perfection. The Buddha was perfection. Mahatma Gandhi was perfection. Nelson Mandela was perfection. The Dali Lama is perfection. Those who live every moment as an expression of their heart define real human perfection. A beauty of the spirit. It is the only perfection, the only beauty, worth emulating. Everything else is just a construct of the linear mind.

Path Finder
Joining a Path

"You told me once that we shall be judged by our intentions, not by our accomplishments. I thought it a grand remark. But we must intend to accomplish– not sit intending on a chair."

~ E. M. Forster, *Where Angels Fear to Tread*

Your first task is to find others who share the same path, or who have the same intention. Even if yours is a singular task such as was the writing of this book, it is vital that it be shared with others. We are a social species, and we work best when we are aligned with others for a common purpose. For this book, I was blessed by those whose help I asked, and by those who asked to be included that I did not know to ask. I have been the pen, but they are also the writers.

First, you must make the call for help, whether it is by a press release or public service announcement, through social media, by word of mouth, or by just asking people you respect. Whether you invite someone or they invite you, you must first be certain that you are aligned in your values. This will take you back to your principles. Be sure you are committed to the same or closely similar principles before you start working together. When you find one or more people on the same path, discuss the project you have in mind, taking any input given with the utmost respect and then come to common ground. From there, one by one, add to the group using the same process. Do not neglect this alignment process. Your risk of failure greatly increases if some join the group who are not committed to its principles.

When you have people with the skills, knowledge and commitment needed to take action, spend time with each other and share your aspirations. These people are your comrades, your best friends and you will need to count on each other to accomplish that which you seek, so hold nothing back. If you are not completely open with each other, or if some of you are still asleep, tread carefully. Motivations, acted on through the lens of beliefs, have foundered many a great idea. Being fully awake makes it easier to discern the difference.

When acting on your intention, you may come up against many obstacles in following your path. The obstacles may take the form of poor communication, prejudice, self interest, hidden agendas, incompetence, ignorance, or active resistance. All of these obstacles may or may not be overcome when taking action. When they cannot be overcome, it is not the time to abandon your intention. it is time to devise a new action. It may mean *"upping the ante,"* either in the action you take, or finding others who may support your effort, or in redefining your intention to improve its success. It may mean dramatically changing the coarse of your actions. In the end, there is no room for hope, faith, or wishful thinking. Just follow your heart, be clear on your intention and take whatever actions you heart deems necessary.

Newly awakened leaders will arise from your ranks, bringing different skills and knowledge sets to the table. Some newly awakened leaders may focus on research, others on communication, others on implementation. Others might have skills in bringing groups to common ground, some might have public speaking skills and others who are skillful at planning, etc. Leaders who, from their hearts, are willing do whatever needs to be done.

A Path with Too Many Choices

One difficulty you may have is that there is more that needs to be done than hours in your day. That is why you need to choose your path wisely. For instance, if child poverty is where you are most called, but you are also called to act on global warming, pollution and species extinctions, how do you proceed?

First of all, you need to decide which area, or areas, you are intuitively drawn to take a leading role. If it is child poverty, then the process is simple. Devote as much time on child poverty as is possible, and then take a supporting role with the rest. You may still be able to attend demonstrations, but you may not be able to do more than that. Remember, others awake people will rise to the occasion.

What you can do, is make lifestyle changes, such as decreasing the carbon footprint in your life, donating to groups serving the areas you support, and talking with your family and friends about what needs to be done. You can also share your concerns with your community, and what you are personally doing as a corrective. Do not proselytize, rather speak from your heart. Tell your neighbors of your concerns and what you are doing, and the urgency you feel. Also, ask them how they feel about the issue, and what they are doing. It could bring you closer.

Of course, you may determine that all of the areas of most concern to you might fit under a larger umbrella. Certainly, global warming, species extinction and pollution, are all related to underlying deficits in humanity's choices. Rather than working on those symptoms, your path might be to help others to awaken. That way you would be releasing many more birds than your hands could ever hold.

Dealing with Push-back

When you take action, your path may lead to push-back from those whose livelihood, wealth, or power is threatened by the cause you advocate. Some of these people will be blinded to your cause, and may be in passive or active resistance. If the push-back comes from those whose wealth or power is at stake, tread lightly, and avoid direct confrontation. Do not allow yourself to fall back on old beliefs and the posing of enemies. *Do not argue with those asleep. Rather, feel compassion for their blindness.* Seeking common ground, peaceful protest, and perhaps legal action, maybe a preferred course. If those in opposition are the wealthy and powerful, use you protest and communications to point to the value of the Earth and her creatures, and the harm caused by their actions. You may not win many points with them, for often the wealthy and powerful are the deepest sleepers.

Your primary aim is to awaken those who toil in their service. Express the deepest compassion for the workers whose livelihood are threatened by the changes ahead. They played by the elites rules, and it is now they who might suffer the most. Hold these people close. Help and support them however you can. Work with them to come up with ways they can transition to a more Earth friendly occupation. Use your occupation as an example. Help them to downsize when possible. In all of this, lead by example.

Work with your local community to develop job training programs. Work with co-operative banks to restructure or forgive debt. If you are able to ease the burden and transition of those most affected, you may even be of aid in their awakening, and you may well gain an ally and a friend.

One of the benefits of being awake is that while your intention remains clear, your actions are fluid. You, and those with you, may find a path through, or around almost any obstacle.

Leaders for Tomorrow – Part Two

Once humanity has thrown off the shackles of belief, and set its course to restoration, a new kind of leader, and a new kind of society will be required. For us to succeed, humanity must transition to a smaller footprint on the Earth. Over the next century, this means a gentle, but substantial reduction in our numbers. The carrying capacity of the Earth, with ample room for all species, has already been greatly exceeded. We must correct this imbalance as quickly as possible. It will mean smaller groupings of our species, sourcing most of our food and materials locally, developing much more efficient transportation systems, transitioning to a low carbon and methane food supply, converting to renewable energy sources, and most importantly, the creation of communities that are in balance with nature, communities that do not have consumption and personal wealth at their core, societies that serve the needs of all their members. The key to this is the leaders born to these new societies. Leaders not recovering from false belief, but leaders who never felt the chains of belief at all. The sons and daughters of our sons and daughters. What a world they might create.

As we work to restore the Earth, we will all have the opportunity to let go together of lingering belief and shared stories that have, in the past, blinded us to our own actions. We will abandon old ways and old selves. We will become the stewards of our worst impulses, and let go those who would divide us. By forming principled communities addressing the needs of the Earth, we will create new ways for people to interact with each other, and to the world. We will change the ecology and the evolutionary direction of humankind. All of us serving the Earth, with no one left out. Communities will coalesce and work together, sharing ideas and visions for a harmonious world without wars, pollution or discord. Because we will be awake, the human race will find its rightful place in the panoply of life.

Political and economic philosophies devoted solely to growth, and perpetuated by the unawakened leaders who brought the Earth to crisis will be dismantled. New political, economic and perhaps spiritual systems will be necessary. The new systems can only be devised by those who have never slept, those ready to serve not just a single species, but all of life.

Steps to Change the World

Once you are on your path to creating a more perfect world you, and those sharing the same path, will need tools. Tools that make your job easier. Tools that help you to act effectively and to help you to become successful.

Structure

The first tool that you will need, and one that many people distrust, is structure. Structure can be a two-edged sword. A structure can help you to act effectively, or if poorly built, can limit your effectiveness. That said, a structure must constantly be evaluated to prevent it becoming dogmatic or bureaucratic in nature. Structure for structure's sake. Structure that serves you is what you are after. The follow guidelines are an example of a structure that might produce effective action.

Define

Define the problem that we wish to address. Whether it is a global warming, or unequal access to justice or pollution, you must be able to clearly state what it is that needs change, and why it is contrary to your principles. Second you must look at the roots of the problem. Are there underlying issues that must be dealt with to eradicate it? How did it come about? If it was caused by legislation, was the legislation meant to address one problem but ended up causing another? If you attack a surface issue, but neglect its underlying causes, you will not succeed.

Research

Look for successful and unsuccessful examples historically that had similarities to the current circumstances. Did they succeed or fail? Why? For example why were Gandhi's and Mandela's causes successful? And why did Arab Spring fail in Egypt? What were the counter forces that allied against the them? What was the state of affairs or conditions that let up to the problem being resolved? You must know why certain actions were successful and why others failed and whether those solutions transfer to your cause?

Understanding

Understanding is taking all the information you have gathered and organizing it into a form that is useful, and worthwhile. It is essential to both know what happened previous to this moment in all its layers and depth, but also what the ramifications are in the present circumstances.

Wisdom

Today, we seldom see wisdom in leaders. At best, we settle for agreement. Most of our leaders are very good at agreement, but are very bad when it comes to clear understanding or making wise choices. Wisdom is essential, for it is most responsible for determining the ultimate successful or failure of any plan or objective. Wisdom is our ability to sift through information and to intuitively pull out the key points, to see patterns and to find solutions. It is the ability to look at an issue and to accurately determine its causes and the degree to which action will be needed. It is the capacity to choose the right course for the right problem at the right time. It is knowing when to fight and when to retreat.

Vision

Vision is harder to define. While wisdom is grounded in large part in intuition and seeing connections in disparate information, vision is based more on the heart. Vision is what we want to make happen and a commitment to realizing it. Vision gives us direction and optimism in the face of fear and dread. Vision says yes when the world tells us no. Vision and wisdom are also interlocked. Wisdom needs the compassion that vision brings. Vision needs the practicality of wisdom to guide it. They are interdependent and vital to success. Never underestimate the value of either.

Planning

Once wise council has been achieved and a vision unites your compatriots, it is time for a plan of action. Planning must be detailed, comprehensive and include all contingencies. It must be based on the strength of your numbers as well as the strength of your adversaries. Planning will fail if it is based solely on what we want. It must be based also on what you know and more important, what you do not know. It must also be flexible to meet changing situations and expectations. Everyone involved must be committed to the action and have the skills to achieve it.

Action

Action has to be specific, targeted and result oriented. Action must have a high likelihood of success, even if success is defined as only raising awareness, or making citizens realize just how hot the water is getting.

Evaluation

Following your action you must determine if you obtained the result you sought. Was the action successful? Did it meet your goals? Did you address the right issue, or was there an underlying issue that caused the problem to persist? Look for creeping dogma. Dogma should be evaluated and cleansed from your thinking on a regular basis to ensure it does not put you or your group back to sleep.

Creating an Intention

A great and loving intention begins as a newborn thought, alone, and yet, a miraculous birth in the intuitive mind may take hold.

When all can see the perfection of the intention,
it begins releasing long held beliefs formerly held close.

If the intention is noble and pure, it will move mountains of beliefs aside, taking mountains of despair with them.

Like a mighty waterfall, whose spray brings forth new life upon it banks,
the intention brings promise and purpose and rebirth to our lives.

As the mountains of beliefs subside, and the river of purpose overflows its banks, we free ourselves of doubt.
and awaken to the glimmering of new intentions.

The mingling of our intentions nurture, and may even supplant the original thought, to releases still greater offshoots of possibility until humanity unfolds, to become the steward, the caretaker, the friend, and lover of all life, and in rapturous love with our only home.

Epilogue

"There is pleasure in the pathless woods,
 there is rapture in the lonely shore,
  there is society where none intrudes,
   by the deep sea, and music in its roar;
    I love not man the less, but nature more."
     ~ George Gordon Byron

The Awakened World
Choices

Nature abhors a vacuum, as does the human mind. We are always seeking answers to mysteries. Usually we have four choices when confronted by mysteries; we can seek an answer through careful study, we can make up an answer, we can simply become a witness to the mystery, or we can ignore what our senses perceive. I will not say anything further about the fourth choice, because that choice is to not choose.

The First Choice

The first choice puts us into action. After careful study, we might pose some hypotheses and attempt to verify if the hypotheses are confirmed by tests we develop. If a hypotheses fails to be confirmed, we can continue to seek other hypotheses, and test them. We may eventually find a hypothesis that is confirmed, and reconfirmed by others. We can then say, with a fair amount of certainty, that the mystery is solved. If none of the hypotheses are able to be confirmed, we may soldier on, and continue proposing new ones, until exhaustion or death takes choice away. This is the scientific method.

The Second Choice

The second choice, telling a story about the mystery, provides answers, as well. Telling a story has power. A good story may last for centuries or even millennia. An obvious example is astrology. Astrology may have been well intentioned, and did influence the live of its adherents through the act of believing. Kind of like the placebo effect, or like a tail wagging a dog.

The Third Choice

What happens though, when no hypothesis or story yields a satisfactory answer? If one cannot come up with a satisfactory answer, using the scientific method or through the making up of a new story, then what? This leads us to the third choice, to becoming a witness.

Becoming a witness does not mean that you are standing idly by, staring into space. The data we receive through all our senses is still being processed and your global thinking intuitive mind is not asleep. Becoming a witness is to be present to phenomena, without belief or supposition, simply acknowledging what our eyes see, what our ears hear, what our minds perceive.

This choice might be our first choice as well, depending upon our disposition. It may be a part of any investigation into a mystery, and it is the foundation of rigorous scientific investigations. It requires the scientist to have no prejudice, or beliefs that might taint their experimental tests. Sadly, not all scientists adhere to these critical requirements, and fall into the category of those making up stories. True understanding can be complicated by many factors, not the least of which is our busy minds, eagerly seeking answers at any cost, willing to ignore any truths that might contradict the answers we seek.

The greatest advantage that the third choice offers is that it allows us to be in the moment, directly connected to our own existence, and to those we hold dear.

Everyday Mysteries

And then there are mysteries where no science or belief is available to provide adequate explanation. Everyday mysteries. Like where did that sock disappear, or what is that cicada doing inside my shopping bag? Why did that feather fall out of the sky and land in my wife's open hand? For that matter, why is that cat bowing to my wife? Why is that bird singing to us at our open window? And what is that chilly praying mantis doing in my refrigerator?

Though mostly ignored, all of us have witnessed these little mysteries. Unexplainable occurrences with no answers. Only there to be witnessed. Perhaps random hiccups in the fabric of time and space. Perhaps a mystery that is a part of a larger mystery. But for now, they remain unknown. For now, they leave us in a state of wonderment, and nothing more. These everyday mysteries are the mysteries I like most. They are unknown, and perhaps unknowable, and they always bring a smile to my face.

A New Age

We are at the beginning of a new age. Humanity must now choose, consciously or unconsciously, the path we will travel together. Probabilities, based on past behaviors, do not look encouraging for this endeavor. But probability is not fate. A person spending decades in debauchery and drunkenness might suddenly awaken, and set a new course in their life. So too, a species filled with self-aggrandizement, plunder and trapped by ancient stories of gods and dreams of dominion, may also suddenly awaken. In truth, many societies have awakened and changed course. Past societies have found ways to end internecine squabbles, to live in harmony with their environment, to find peace. Not often, but when the stakes were high enough, the likelihood of such shifts was greatly increased. Many societies however, could not turn away from their beliefs and are now gone, as Percy Bysshe Shelley's poem Ozymandias reminds us:

Ozymandias

"I met a traveler from an antique land,

Who said, 'Two vast and trunkless legs of stone

Stand in the desert... Near them, on the sand,

Half sunk a shattered visage lies, whose frown,

And wrinkled lip, and sneer of cold command,

Tell that its sculptor well those passions read

Which yet survive, stamped on these lifeless things,

The hand that mocked them, and the heart that fed;

And on the pedestal, these words appear:

> 'My name is Ozymandias, King of Kings;
>
> Look on my works, ye Mighty, and despair!'
>
> Nothing beside remains. Round the decay
>
> Of that colossal wreck, boundless and bare
>
> The lone and level sands stretch far away."

In the coming decade, humanity's decisions and choices will set the course for life on Earth for eons to come. We cannot allow Shelley's dark vision to foretell the fate of humanity, but it is certainly one of the possibilities, if we do not choose a different path than the one we have followed up until now.

- Do we choose a course that leads us out of that desert of despair into a future of harmony and balance?
- Do we choose harmony, even if it means giving up e n e m i e s?
- Do we choose balance, even though the cost is our beliefs?
- Can we share all that we have, that all life may live, even if it means the end of greed and self-interest?
- Do we give up adrenalized lives that keep us from following our hearts, even if it means we have to slow down and *smell the roses*?
- Do we give up unsustainable growth, even if it means humans have a smaller footprint upon the earth?
- Can we choose the kind loving leaders that our old leaders were not?
- And can we awaken everyone?

These rhetorical questions must be answered in the affirmative. Our paths are clear. We must lovingly act, together. The time has come for us to welcome awakened humanity.

ACKNOWLEDGEMENTS
My Three Muses

Three Editors, Three Confidants

I had the help of three editors and confidants, without whose guidance, this book would not have been possible.

Thank you to Ronna Pomeroy for your loving care, for holding my hand, for making me dig deeper, and for helping me take this book from idle musings and rumination spinning in my head to a reality that greatly exceeded what I thought possible.

Thank you to Carol Barrick-Murillo for allowing me to take advantage of your bright spirit and mind, for your critical, but gentle eye, for challenging my fuzzy thinking and for your wise counsel, as you continue on *your* path.

Thank you to Allen Gomes for your kind encouragement and wisdom, for bringing light to this quest, and for the renewal of an old friendship.

Thank you also, my dear muses, for your forbearance and for putting up with the thousand changes I made along the way, as I kept shifting directions, refining tone and adding new material from the beginning of the project to the end. You were not just muses, you were saints, and I am forever in your debt.

There are many more who helped whom I have not mentioned. To those, my dear friends, thank you also, for serving as my guides and inspiration.

ABOUT

John Elmer Lee

A Brief History

John was a war baby.
John was a child.
John was a student.
John was a lover.
John was a husband.
John was a parent.
John was a brother
John was a friend.
John was a slave to wages.
John was a slave to dreams.
John was a mechanic.
John was a motorcycle racer.
John was a mushroom picker.
John was a failure.

John was a protester.
John was a blogger.
John was a button maker.
John was a manager.
John was a director.
John was a sculptor.
John was a photographer.
John was a writer
John was a publisher.
John was a seeker.
John was a hater.
All these infatuations John has ceased to entertain.
Today, John is only his heart.
Today, John is reawakening...

ABOUT
Johnny Peaceseed

"In the land of Nod the heart is just like a spiel, the more you speak, the less you feel."
　　　　　　　　~ Johnny Peaceseed, Momentary Memoirs

Johnny's Awakening
The History of Johnny Peaceseed

In the Spring of 2003 Johnny Peaceseed was born. Johnny Peaceseed was to be my alter-ego. The name was chosen as I struggled with the hypocrisies of war, and how I might contribute to the peace movement. The name allowed me to step out of my skin, and any reluctance I might feel about standing out in a crowd. Johnny allowed me to make speeches on the steps of the legislature, to design and distribute t-shirts and buttons, to write blogs, to become comfortable outside my comfort zone. Johnny was born out of anger and frustration at the willingness of my fellows to join the chorus for war. At the time, I often wrote of peace, but anger was my engine. How could we not see through the lies and propaganda urging war?

Eventually, I turned my gaze to unfounded belief, and saw that it was the ultimate engine that kept humanity in a perpetual state of unrest, uncertainty and the willingness to follow heartless paths. I saw that, in our reliance on language, belief was a fundamentally overarching false path. I did not write of this for many years because it took many years to fully realize the implications of that awareness, and how deeply encompassing humanity's attachment to belief has become.

In July of this year I reawakened my alter-ego Johnny. Only not as the firebrand, full of blame and recrimination, but as the one who had been born forty-seven years ago, the lost and then found lover.

On the First of July of 2019, I started the writing of this book. In those forty-seven years learned that anger begets anger, that hate begets hate, that selfishness creates loneliness and that love is always the answer. That love is all that we humans possess that will allow the restoration of balance. Loving ourselves, loving humankind with all our flaws. Loving the Earth and all that lives upon her.

As one who was awakened and who flirted with enlightenment for many years, I can finally say I are back on the path. Love has healed my heart. I are gratefully still alert, and I am ready to tilt at the windmills of belief once more. In the past, what kept me from remaining awake continuously was inconsistency in my practices, losing my way for a while, and getting lost in another's suffering.

I finally realized that the lack of discipline was most responsible for my erratic journey. I had spun my metaphorical wheels, until the day I finally decided to stop flirting, and started to develop the practices and disciplines necessary to stay awake. In spite of my turbulent journey, I cherish each moment of clarity, and the abiding purpose that still guides me. I can expect no more.

It is my intention to plant seeds of peace wherever I can, and to follow a path with heart as long as I live.

Johnny's Perfect World

"We live in paradise if we have the eyes to see it."
~ Johnny Peaceseed, Momentary Memoirs

What constitutes a perfect, unblemished world? I ask this, not as some wishful speculation, but as an examination of what an enlightened human society might look like, what it would take for humanity to get from here to there. I begin with a draft of what a perfect world might include:

People are awake from birth onward. Communities are structured so humanity is not left to flounder in unfounded belief.

If there are leaders, they are chosen based on the size of their heart and the degree of their enlightenment.

The leaders tell the truth, the whole truth and nothing but the truth.

The size of your heart matters more than the size of your wallet.

The depth of your character matter more than your desires.

Those honored by the community are those who give the most, not those who take the most.

Peace is sought as vigorously as war and violence were in the past.

The "Commons" refers to the whole of the Earth.

People are educated and understand the implications of any solutions proposed to address the needs of the community.

Communication is unfettered and is focused only on seeking truth, understanding and wisdom.

Individuals limit their childbearing to that which is sustainable for the Earth.

All children are treated with love and respect by their parents and by their community.

Economic systems take into account the Earth and all her inhabitants in the costing of human activities.

Respect for the environment and its non-human inhabitants is given a higher value than any human dreams of wealth.

All development is sustainable without degrading global ecological systems.

Economic wealth is shared equally by all in the community.

Individual spiritual wealth is shared and reciprocated by all.

There are no enemies, only friends.

Free trade means fair wages, healthy working conditions and environmentally sound practices free of exploitation, child labor, prison labor and the destruction of native cultures. For that matter, there will be no need for prisons, militarism or endless growth economics.

Greed is, once again, considered a sin.

Do unto others as you would have done unto you applies to all foreign and domestic policies.

My list for a Perfect World is far from complete, but it is something I use when I make my daily choices about what I buy, which candidate I endorse, which policies I support and how I treat my fellow beings. I'm sure the list will change with time. I'm also sure that my yearning for a just, equitable and peaceful world will not.

www.ingramcontent.com/pod-product-compliance
Lightning Source LLC
Chambersburg PA
CBHW071523080526
44588CB00011B/1544